# Blue-Collar Leadership® & Teamwork:
# 30 Traits of High Impact Players

Mack Story

# DEDICATION

To the high impact player who made the most positive
impact on my life and taught me the most about
teamwork, my amazing wife Ria Story. You have always
been and will always be the wind beneath my wings.
You helped turn my Blue-Collar Leadership® idea into an
amazing Blue-Collar Leadership® brand.

# CONTENTS

# ACKNOWLEDGMENTS

I would like to thank the high impact players I've been privileged to serve alongside. Many of the lessons I'm about to share were learned from you. Although you may not have literally taught the lessons, I still caught the lessons.

# TRAIT 1

## BE GROWTH-ORIENTED

### WHEN YOU GROW YOURSELF,
### YOU GROW YOUR INFLUENCE

*"Intellectual growth should commence at birth and cease only at death." ~ Albert Einstein*

Why should you focus on growth? Because growth creates freedom and options, and your life will always be better with more freedom and more options. When the team creates more options for the organization, everyone will benefit. When the leaders create more options for the team, the team will benefit.

When you, your team, or your organization are out of options, life isn't getting better. It's getting worse.

When you grow, the team automatically grows. You can't grow yourself without growing your team because you are a part of the team. If you want the team to be better, the quickest way you can make that happen is to take the lead and get better yourself.

Too many people are goal-oriented. The problem with being goal-oriented is that when you reach your goal you're done. Mission accomplished. You no longer have a need to grow. Unfortunately, when this happens, most begin coasting and stop growing. The key is to be growth-oriented first and goal-oriented second. In this manner, you're always setting new goals to facilitate your overall mission: continued growth.

The foundation of growth is discipline. The foundation of discipline is sacrifice. Sacrifice creates the opportunity for growth, but it does not create the growth. When you sacrifice, you're giving up something such as time or money normally spent on other things and valued activities. Giving these things up doesn't cause you to grow. The sacrifice must be leveraged with discipline. You must have the discipline to use your recovered time and money to invest in your personal growth and development. This takes discipline. Only discipline will allow you to convert the sacrifice into growth.

SACRIFICE + DISCIPLINE = GROWTH

Charles Schulz remarked, "Life is like a ten-speed bike. Most of us have gears we never use." I agree. I meet a lot of people who aren't using all of their gears. Low impact players tend to settle on getting by instead of getting ahead. High impact players are always focused on climbing to the next level and beyond.

When it comes to growth, high impact players are focused not only on personal growth, but also on leadership development. They understand leadership in its simplest form is authentic influence which is based on a person's character, not their position, title, rank, or authority. High impact players see themselves and all of their teammates as leaders who should be developed.

All team members are required to develop their competency in order to do their job. But, seldom are team members required to develop their character. High impact players always do more than required. Reading leadership books, listening to leadership audios, and watching leadership videos are ways they grow themselves in an effort to position themselves to grow their team.

To help with my storytelling throughout this book, I want to introduce you to Blue-Collar Bob. He's not a real person, but rather a character I've created. At times, you may see yourself in Bob. Other times, you may see those you know in Bob.

Like the rest of us, Bob gets it right sometimes. Other times, he gets it wrong. But either way, we can learn from Bob. If we will simply look for the lessons, we'll discover everyone is capable of teaching us something.

One morning, Bob noticed a quote posted on the bulletin board at work. He had never noticed quotes on the board before. "Wonder who put that there?" he thought as he began to read the words of Mark Twain, "I have never let my schooling interfere with my education."

Bob found Twain's words thought provoking. It took him a few minutes to figure out the meaning in Twain's message. Then, it finally hit him as he thought to himself, "Schooling and education are two completely different things. We get our formal schooling in traditional K-12 schools, technical colleges, and universities, but we get our 'education' throughout our lives."

Bob reflected on his life and realized he had been relying too much on his "schooling" and hadn't been focused enough on his "education." He thought to himself, "I haven't even read a book from cover to cover since I finished school and that was years ago." When Bob was no longer required to read books, he did what most people do. He stopped reading books.

Bob made his way to his work area and kept busy the rest of the day. However, Twain's words stayed with him. He was thinking about his "education" and wondered, "If I get serious about my 'education,' what will change? Can I improve? Should I improve? How can I improve?"

*"You don't have to be sick to get better."*
*~ Michael Josephson*

3

# Trait 2

## BE TRUSTWORTHY

### YOUR CHARACTER WILL EITHER LAUNCH YOU OR LIMIT YOU

*"What you really are will speak so loudly that what you 'claim' you are will not be heard."*
*~ Napoleon Hill*

With trust, we have much influence; without trust, we have little influence. With trust, team morale is high; without trust, team morale is low. With trust, we work together; without trust, we work separately. With trust, the mission is likely to be accomplished; without trust, the mission is likely to be compromised.

When it comes to high performing blue-collar teams, there's one thing I know for certain: Trust is the one thing that impacts everything.

You can't make someone trust you. I can't make someone trust me. It simply isn't possible. What is possible? Consistently making choices that make us trustworthy people. Ultimately, you must choose to be trustworthy; I must choose to be trustworthy.

Trust is the foundation upon which high impact teams thrive. Each player, regardless of their position, title, or rank is responsible for intentionally helping the team build a strong foundation of trust. The principles you'll discover on these pages, if applied, will help anyone at any level become a high impact team player.

My blue-collar career started on the front lines of a manufacturing plant in 1988 operating a large, hot, dirty, and extremely oily vertical broach. I learned to operate many types of machines over the next 10 years. Then, I began to be promoted into various support roles where I continued to work with those on the front lines.

For the first 10 years, I had basically been an individual contributor on a big team. To succeed, all I had to do was meet or exceed my production goals while working by myself on my machine. I wasn't part of an official team or committee. Building trust for me was about getting individual results. I simply had to perform and produce.

When I began to be promoted, everything changed.

In the support roles, I had to work with and through others. I also started to be assigned to various types of teams. No longer was my success based primarily on my knowledge, skills, and abilities. To be effective, I had to establish trust while working with others which meant I had to be seen as trustworthy. And, others had to establish trust with me. Trust is a two-way street.

At that point in my career, my success began to be based on my ability to build relationships. My success started with me, but it was no longer about me. As the years progressed, I began accepting opportunities to lead teams. Not only did I have to continue building trust, but I had to start helping others learn to build trust.

Between 2005 and 2012, I logged over 11,000 hours in blue-collar industries leading leaders and their cross-functional teams through process improvement, organizational change, and cultural transformation. As a result, I learned many lessons from many people. I've written this book to help you become more valuable and successful as you think deeply about the choices that will make you a trustworthy high impact team player.

In 2008, I started reading leadership development and personal growth books daily to accelerate my own journey to the next level and beyond. In 2014, I started writing my own books to help people like you make a bigger impact. In 2016, I started writing books specifically for those in the blue-collar workforce who have traditionally been overlooked, underappreciated, and underdeveloped. All 12 of my books are filled with principles that will help you "Be Trustworthy."

I've discovered the majority of those in the blue-collar workforce are hungry for development. Most have never been exposed to this type of content. This book is another attempt to feed those who are hungry. Those who want to intentionally turn it up a notch by focusing on developing the traits that lead to high trust relationships.

Trust is based on two things: 1) a person's character; who they are; and 2) a person's competency; what they know. Numerous studies have revealed our character is responsible for 87-90% of our ability to build trust, and our competency is responsible for only 10-13%. All of my books focus on character development. When it comes to trust, character counts.

"Be Trustworthy" is the most important trait. However, this one trait is based upon many other traits. In each of the following chapters, I'll share a trait that will help you "Be Trustworthy." There are seemingly endless character traits that will make you a trustworthy person. While leading thousands of blue-collar team members, I've validated these 30 key traits many times. Learn and embrace them, and you will "Be Trustworthy."

*"I judge myself by my best intentions, but others judge me by my worst acts." ~ Michael Josephson*

# TRAIT 3

## BE HUMBLE

### YOUR LEVEL OF HUMILITY
### REVEALS YOUR LEVEL OF SECURITY

*"Humility is the mother of all virtues because humility acknowledges that there are natural laws and principles that govern the universe.*
*They are in charge. We are not.*
*Pride teaches us that we are in charge.*
*Humility teaches us to understand and live by principles, because they ultimately govern the consequences of our actions. If humility is the mother, courage is the father of wisdom. Because to truly live by these principles when they are contrary to social mores, norms, and values takes enormous courage."*
*~ Stephen R. Covey*

My wife, Ria, had the privilege of speaking to a large group of prison wardens to kick off a nine month Transformational Leadership development program near San Francisco, California in January 2017. I was privileged and excited to also receive an invitation to attend the two day kick-off.

The focus of the entire program was to help the wardens learn how to grow and develop their support teams. Ultimately, the goal was for them to develop high impact players. The key to growing and developing high impact team players is to be a high impact team player yourself which is exactly what the wardens would be focused on during the nine month program.

While we were there, we got to meet and invest some time with retired Prison Warden Burl Cain. Cain had been the warden at the Louisiana State Penitentiary at Angola from 1995-2016. Angola was home to over 5,000 inmates at times and was once referred to as the bloodiest prison in America. However, Cain led an unprecedented transformation at Angola. As Dennis Shere, author of *Cain's Redemption,* wrote, "Angola is now known as a place of hope."

What I remember most about Warden Cain is his humility. Yes, he was the Warden. But more importantly, he was a high impact player on a high impact team. I'll never forget his simple message to the other wardens gathered there that day.

Cain said, "Be humble, so you don't stumble." That was Cain's personal motto. I saw him model it effortlessly for two days straight. When we're not humble, there's no doubt we're more likely to stumble.

When Cain took over Angola, he had too much pride. His pride not only had a negative impact on him, but it also negatively impacted his team. As Ezra Taft Benson stated so well, "Pride is concerned with who is right. Humility is concerned with what is right."

Fortunately for Warden Cain and his team, he quickly turned the corner by learning to set his pride aside and focus on doing what was right, not on being right.

Players who want to be seen as right are focused on themselves and have a "me" focus. Those focused on doing what's right are focused on others and have a "we" focus.

A team suffers when their efforts must revolve around a low impact player's pride and ego. The prideful player also suffers. However, they often suffer in the dark. They're unaware of how much their character flaws are holding them back.

The low impact player doesn't realize how their influence is diminished as a result. Because those who are prideful and driven by ego tend to always be that way, they don't know what they don't know. They see humility as a weakness, not as a strength.

Too much pride and ego are indicators of insecurity. The most insecure among us are also the least humble among us. Insecure people try to prove something on the outside to make up for what's missing on the inside.

High impact players are always humble. They don't want credit. But, they do want to give credit to others. They don't want the spotlight on themselves and prefer to shine the spotlight on others.

Ria and I had the privilege of investing a full day training and developing a Blue-Collar CEO and his entire staff and manufacturing team recently. The moment I met the CEO, I knew he was a humble, high impact player. He was wearing the same uniform the front line team members were wearing. He spoke highly of those on the front lines and avoided speaking about himself. He sat through every development session, even those that were repeated, and took more notes than anyone else.

Humility has nothing to do with position, title, and rank. Humility has everything to do with character.

*"The best thing we can do is be who we are, whatever that is. We're all drawn to authenticity. We like people who are real. Sometimes real people are flawed, we're all flawed. I think we connect with people who are open, exposed, willing to admit things they're good at, things they're not good at, try to be humble, try to be collaborative." ~ Bob Myers*

# TRAIT 4

## BE RESPONSIBLE

### MAKING THIS CHOICE GIVES YOU A VOICE

*"Total responsibility for failure is a difficult thing to accept, and taking ownership when things go wrong requires extraordinary humility and courage."*
*~ Jocko Willink*

If we haven't done much or accomplished much, it's easier to remain humble. But, the higher we climb up the organizational chart or the higher we climb up the pay scale, the harder it is for many of us to remain humble. As high impact team players, it's our responsibility to choose to be humble regardless of our status or income. And if necessary, it's also our responsibility to learn what it truly means to be humble. Being humble is a choice high impact players make.

I believe as a whole the blue-collar workforce is naturally more humble simply because of who we are and where we come from. However, I also believe some who have climbed their way up from entry-level positions let success go to their heads.

Not letting my success go to my head is my responsibility. I want to remain a humble high impact player. That's on me. High impact team players always do more than is required, so I've also gone a step farther and made helping others do the same my responsibility.

Each of us is responsible for choosing our values and

those values will determine our circumstances and the impact we have, especially when it comes to teamwork.

Just as humility is sometimes a hard choice for those with a high position or status, taking responsibility is often a hard choice for those in a low position or status. But as I've learned over the years, taking responsibility seems to be a hard choice for many regardless of their title, position, rank, status, or income.

When it comes to teamwork, low impact players dodge responsibility like it's a deadly disease. They may disappear when a task is being addressed or begin to make excuses as to why they can't help and shouldn't be asked to help. Lack of responsibility creates distrust.

High impact players know a secret: When low impact players are whining, it's easy to start shining. They also know how to shine. It's actually pretty simple. They just listen for whining, and then step up and say, "I'll do it."

At that moment, the high impact player builds trust by simply taking responsibility. The next responsibility of the high impact player is to follow through and get results. If they do, they will build additional trust with the team and their leaders. If they don't, they will create distrust with the team and their leaders.

Leaders are ultimately responsible for making things happen. If they don't make things happen, it won't be long before they are replaced by someone else who will be given the same mission. High impact players know the quickest way to build trust with a leader is to help them get results, so that's what they focus on doing.

As they develop a reputation for helping their leaders get results, their influence also increases with other leaders. Because of their choice (taking responsibility and following through), they earn a voice. As time passes, high impact players are asked their opinion much more often than low impact players.

As a result, high impact players begin to influence the leader's choices and the team's direction. Those who are willing to make things happen are also given more chances to make things happen. They're still on the team, but they're playing at a much higher level.

High impact players are never just along for the ride. They want to drive. They see the big picture. They don't shy away from responsibility. They wake up every day looking for an opportunity to shine.

Imagine a team full of low impact players where everyone is dodging responsibility on every front. The leader will be frustrated, and the team will be frustrated. And little, if anything, will be accomplished. Unfortunately, these types of teams are common. Depending on your circumstances, it may be too easy to imagine this team. If so, don't miss what's right in front of you: endless opportunities to shine.

Now imagine a very different team, one filled with high impact players. They could be given the exact same mission as the frustrated low impact team. However, no one would be frustrated. The mission would be accomplished. Instead of being focused on finding excuses, the entire team would be focused on finding a way to make it happen. In that case, everyone shines.

What's the major difference between the two teams above? Attitude. Low impact players tend to have a negative attitude. High impact players tend to have a positive attitude. Attitude is a choice. If we can choose to be positive or negative, why not choose to be positive?

*"Responsibility includes two important ideas – choosing right over wrong and accepting ownership for one's conduct and obligations." ~ Charles G. Koch*

# TRAIT 5

## BE POSITIVE

### THOSE WHO WHINE GET LEFT BEHIND

*"People have just two choices when it comes to their emotions: they can master their emotions or be mastered by them." ~ John C. Maxwell*

Your emotions matter. They can make you or break you. Consider again where your authentic influence comes from: 87% character (who you are) and 13% competency (what you know). You can easily validate this by reflecting on what you've likely witnessed in the work place because people tend to be hired for what they know: their skills, knowledge, and abilities. However, they tend to be fired for who they are: their attitude, behavior, temper, etc.

When it comes to teamwork, emotions matter a lot because emotions are contagious. Negativity is the most contagious of all. It's easy to catch and easy to spread.

The next time you go into a break room, lunch room, a meeting, or walk up to any group of people, simply listen for a few minutes and see if positivity or negativity has infected the group. The majority of the time, it'll be negativity because negativity is highly contagious.

Negativity infects nearly every team to some degree, some much more than others. When you encounter a group infected with negativity, be careful. You don't want to become infected too. Negativity will have a terrible impact on your career. It reduces your income, makes you less likely to be promoted, minimizes the opportunities that will come your way, and decreases your influence.

When you hear the negativity coming from one person, pay close attention and see if the other people join in (low impact players) or if they attempt to spread some positivity (high impact players). High impact players are easy to spot in a negative crowd. They'll either be silent or "Be Positive."

In many blue-collar break rooms, lunch rooms, and on the factory floors of many manufacturing facilities across the country, I've discovered over the years the negative voices are always the loudest.

If a high impact player tries to spread a little positivity, they'll likely be bombarded with negativity from all the low impact players. Be prepared. You're likely to be outnumbered. That's just the way it is. High impact players are often in the minority.

As Daniel Goleman remarked, "Controlling impulses like frustration and anger is a crucial aspect of character." You can't be frustrated, angry, and positive at the same time. When you choose to "Be Positive," you are saying no to frustration and anger. When you choose to be frustrated and angry, you are saying no to being positive.

Several days had passed since Blue-Collar Bob had received the common-sense lesson on "schooling" and "education" from the legendary 1800's Mississippi River Boat Captain, Mark Twain. Bob was on his way to the bulletin board once again. He discovered something interesting on the board last time, so he thought he would swing by to see if anything new had been posted.

To Bob's surprise, Twain's quote had been taken down. But, it had been replaced with another quote.

Bob began to read these words from Jeffrey Gitomer,

"A positive attitude is a self-imposed blessing."

Bob was often frustrated and angry as he worked hard on the front lines. He had a negative attitude because he didn't have much influence with his team: his boss and the co-workers he interacted with regularly. Bob had all kinds of ideas, but no one would listen to him, much less ask for his opinion.

As Bob walked away from the board and toward his work area, he repeated Gitomer's words, "A positive attitude is a self-imposed blessing." He was trying to decide if the statement was true or not.

What Bob knew for sure was he didn't have a positive attitude. Bob went about his day as usual, glum and downcast. But, he couldn't quit thinking about the quote. Even after work, it was still on his mind. That night, he decided to change his attitude to test out the principle contained in the quote. He knew it wouldn't be easy, but he knew he was missing out on something. "Life shouldn't be so dreary and miserable," he thought to himself, "I'll give it a try."

The next day, Bob approached everyone with a smile and a hello instead of a frown and a growl. He was intentionally positive all day. It was hard, but he did it.

That evening Bob reflected on his day. He was still physically tired from the work, but he wasn't mentally tired from stress. Nothing on the outside had changed, but something on the inside had changed. For the first time in a long time, Bob had a good day. "That was a self-imposed blessing. Be positive." he thought to himself.

*"When morale is low, the only way to get the ball rolling is to start pushing it yourself."*
*~ John C. Maxwell*

# TRAIT 6

## BE FLEXIBLE

### WHEN CHANGE HAPPENS,
### SOME THRIVE AND SOME TAKE A DIVE

*"Live out of your imagination, not your history."*
*~ Stephen R. Covey*

Change. Some embrace it, but most resist it. High impact players intentionally grow through change. In simple terms, they shine. Low impact players angrily go through change. In simple terms, they whine.

As Woodrow Wilson said, "If you want to make enemies, try to change something." When change happens, average players tend to resist. In other words, they choose to be negative. But the truly exceptional players who understand the value of being flexible when change happens, choose to "Be Positive." They intentionally look for the positives related to the change, not the negatives. You will find what you're looking for.

As you're beginning to see, high impact players leverage these traits by combining them when possible to maximize their positive impact on their team and to maximize their influence with the leaders of their team.

As Ria wrote in our book, *Change Happens: Leading Yourself and Others through Change*, "When we leverage something, we take advantage of the lever to multiply the results of our efforts. Leveraging something can be a powerful way to gain momentum and accelerate progress.

But, we seldom think of change as something we can, or should, leverage." Many of the 30 traits found in *Blue-Collar Leadership® & Teamwork* can be used to leverage change for your benefit.

If you want to be seen as a high impact game changer, choose to embrace, support, leverage, and even lead change if you're truly serious about climbing to the next level and beyond. When it comes to your success, don't focus on becoming more successful. Focus on becoming more valuable. Those who help move the team and the organization forward are the most valuable players on the team. Not some of the time, all of the time.

Relative to change, if you're going to be on the team, you can either play or sit on the bench. You'll have a lot more fun on the field in the starting lineup making things happen than you will sitting on the bench waiting to see what happens. Flexibility is another choice that will give you a voice. When change happens, high impact players lead the way. They are flexible, engaged, and looking for ways to make things happen.

After Blue-Collar Bob accepted responsibility for his attitude by testing and validating the theory of embracing a positive attitude, he discovered controlling his emotions was a choice. He could choose to "BE" however he wanted to be.

When Bob began changing on the inside, he noticed things started getting better on the outside. There were still problems, challenges, and issues for him and his team to deal with on a daily basis, but his negative attitude was no longer one of them. As Bob continued to "Be Positive," he began to wish some others would do the same. "They need to be more positive too," he thought.

But, to maintain a positive mindset, Bob didn't focus on everyone else. When he felt like blaming others, he noticed negative feelings started to creep back in. So, he kept his focus on the mirror because he had discovered one opportunity for improvement there and felt there were likely more. Bob had discovered this simple truth: The face we see least is our own.

Several weeks after choosing to "Be Positive," Bob was approached by his boss. "Hi Bob!" the boss said with a handshake and pat on Bob's shoulder. "Hi!" Bob replied with his recently rediscovered smile. "Bob, I've been asked to assemble a team to identify process changes that will allow us to increase our output, so we can meet an increase in demand for our products. I'm hoping you'll volunteer to be on the team."

As the boss was talking, Bob's blood pressure started to rise. He didn't like change, especially change related to his job. He didn't know what to do, but he knew what not to do. "Don't be negative," he thought. Bob said the only positive thing he could come up with, "Sure, I'll be glad to." With a look of surprise, his boss replied, "Thanks, I'll get back with you on the details."

"Now what?" Bob thought. He chose to simply take it one day at a time and one positive choice at a time. In the end, he survived. The team implemented some great ideas, and many of those ideas were Bob's ideas.

The reality: changes were going to be made. They had to get better. In the past, process improvement had been done to Bob because he was resistant. This time, it was done with him because he was flexible and had a positive attitude. Was it easy for Bob? No way. Was it worth it? Every day. All of a sudden, people valued his opinion.

*"Facing reality can be painful and difficult, but the consequences of not confronting it are always far worse." ~ Henry Cloud*

# TRAIT 7

## BE FOCUSED

### MINIMIZING YOUR DISTRACTIONS
### MAXIMIZES YOUR RESULTS

*"Winners concentrate on winning.
Losers concentrate on getting by." ~ Truett Cathy*

You may have heard someone ask, "Are you playing to win? Or, are you playing not to lose?" Whether you've heard it before or this was the first time, you may be wondering, "What's the difference?"

When you're playing to win, you're focused on the big picture. You know who you are and where you are. You also know who you want to become and where you want to be, as an individual, a team, or an organization.

High impact players are focused. They walk into the room with purpose. Regardless of where they are, they are there for a reason. That reason is to make an impact. They are playing to win, and they want to be on a team that's playing to win. These players do far more than is required of them. Are you one of them?

Low impact players aren't focused. They walk into a room hoping to walk out without being assigned a task or being asked to contribute to the conversation. They are there because someone told them to be there. They don't want to be there. They are playing not to lose. They're just happy to have a job. These players do only what's required of them. Are you one of them?

I've led hundreds of focused process improvement teams. Each team as a whole had a very clear focus. However, that didn't mean each team member showed up focused on the big picture. They were all individuals. As a result, some were only focused on themselves.

Some were there because they wanted to be. They volunteered and were more focused on the mission. Some were there only because they were told to be. In other words, they were "voluntold" and most of them weren't focused on anything beyond getting through the week with the least possible effort and involvement.

With this small bit of information, you can easily form an opinion of the two different types of team members often found on various types of cross-functional teams. You may have been on similar teams in the past. You may have volunteered, or you may have been "voluntold." Maybe both at different times for different reasons.

Which type of person is playing to win? The volunteers. Which is playing not to lose? Those who were "voluntold." If you were leading the team, who would you rather have on your team?

It's an easy call to make. The volunteers. At a minimum, the volunteers are focused on moving themselves and the organization forward. Volunteering is one way you can demonstrate a willingness to accept responsibility. It's another way to shine.

When you look in the mirror, do you see someone who volunteers for team based activities and special assignments? Or, do you see someone who must be "voluntold" to participate in team based activities and special assignments? Does your answer increase or decrease your influence with those high impact players at various levels who are ultimately responsible for moving the organization forward? What's the impact?

Some reading this may be thinking, "I was hired to do my job. I'm happy to do it, but I don't want to be on teams. That isn't my job." If you're thinking that, pause and look at the bigger picture because you're playing not to lose, which means you're getting beat on a regular basis by those who are playing to win.

Consider the following. There are all types and sizes of teams. If you work in an organization, you are part of the entire team. If you work in a department, you are a part of the departmental team. If you work on a team assembled for a special project, you are on a cross-functional team. If you live with others, you are part of a family. All of these are teams.

Most people are usually on several teams at once without realizing it. Why? Because they aren't focused on the big picture. They're simply going through the motions of life at work and at home. It doesn't mean they're bad people. It does mean they're not focused people.

Everyone is on a team, but they're not always playing to win. Your team (organization, department, family, etc.) needs you to volunteer to take on more responsibility. When you don't do it, you're letting the team down. When you do it, you're helping the team win.

When you let one of your teams down, you are most often focused on the wrong thing: yourself.

High impact players focus on their team. They know these truths. When the team wins, they win. When the team excels, they excel. When the team is doing well, they are doing well. Where's your focus? Self or team?

*"Man's basic vice...is the act of unfocusing his mind, the suspension of his consciousness, which is not blindness, but the refusal to see, not ignorance, but the refusal to know." ~ Ayn Rand*

# TRAIT 8

## BE DISCIPLINED

### GIVE YOURSELF A COMMAND
### AND FOLLOW THROUGH

*"Today is always the result of actions and decisions taken yesterday." ~ Peter Drucker*

High impact players do what they said they would do, when they said they would do it, how they said they would do it, because they said they would do it. Their words matter. The greater the discipline, the better the player.

We've all worked with team members who make commitments, but seldom, if ever, follow through. They may report to you, you may report to them, they may be on the same level as you, or they may be on a cross-functional team you're leading. Keeping commitments isn't about your title, position, or rank, it's about your character. Ask yourself, "When team members break commitments, do I trust them more or less?"

Now, ask yourself a more important question, "How often do I break commitments? At work? At home? How does this impact my relationships? My influence? My team?"

Making a commitment always reveals your intention. Whether or not you keep that commitment always reveals your character. What separates high impact players from low impact players is their character. High impact players are always asking themselves, "Will what I'm about to do build trust or create distrust?" Their focus is on building trust with as many of their teammates as possible.

When you make commitments, don't make them lightly. Making commitments is important. When you make commitments, you create hope among your teammates. They are counting on you to follow through. When you keep commitments, you build trust. When you break commitments, you create distrust.

Making and keeping commitments is between you and you. Discipline is an inside job. You choose to commit or not to commit. Once committed, you then choose to follow through or to not follow through.

Blue-Collar Bob began to notice someone was changing the quotes on the bulletin board on a daily basis, so he made sure to pass by it at least once a day. Although some quotes didn't seem to apply to him, he found others to be very interesting.

Bob started adding the quotes he liked to a "note" file in his phone, so he could review and reflect on them more deeply when he had time. He also wanted to be able to share them with others later and started posting quotes in his own department. He figured if the quotes were helping him, maybe they would help others too.

One day when Bob went to review the daily quote on the bulletin board, he was impacted greatly by the words he discovered, "The pain of discipline weighs ounces. Regret weighs tons." ~ Jim Rohn

Bob was stunned. Rohn's words cut deep. He had developed his own regrets, and they "weighed tons." He had made enough progress to see how he had been his own worst enemy for years. A little discipline had allowed him to move forward. He thought to himself, "Where would I be in life if I had discovered these principles years ago? What would be different at home? At work?"

With that thought, Bob remembered an old saying he had heard many times. However, now it took on a new meaning, "The best time to have planted a tree you need today was 20 years ago. If you didn't do that but you still need a tree, the second best time to plant it is today." He didn't dwell on the past, but he used it to inspire himself to get busy and stay the course.

Bob had also learned that making disciplined choices to be positive each day wasn't really that hard. In order to keep his commitment to being positive, he had chosen not to focus on the mountain, but rather to focus on each moment.

Bob knew instinctively if he could conquer enough moments, he would eventually conquer the mountain. He focused on being positive, but he was also unknowingly developing a high degree of self-discipline as he continued to make his personal transformation one "ounce" at a time.

As Bob returned to his work area to post the quote on his own board, he wondered what others thought about his transformation. Most had already acknowledged liking the "new" Bob better than the "old" Bob.

However, those who were negative like Bob had been in the past seemed to be distancing themselves from him. That didn't matter to Bob because he was on a mission to make his life better. Regardless of what his teammates thought about his transformation, he knew he was doing the right things for the right reasons.

Discipline allowed Bob to begin reshaping himself and aligning his life around timeless principles.

*"In a culture of discipline, people do not have jobs; they have responsibilities." ~ Jim Collins*

# TRAIT 9

## BE INTENTIONAL

### ACTION TODAY LEADS
### TO OPTIONS TOMORROW

*"Small deeds done are better than
great deeds planned." ~ Peter Marshall*

Being disciplined is closely related to being intentional. However, these are two very different traits. Being disciplined is about making and keeping commitments to yourself and to others. Being intentional is about making and keeping commitments related to specific goals or objectives.

In the early 2000's, I volunteered to lead the entire manufacturing team and the leaders where I worked through a Lean Manufacturing transformation. I made a huge commitment that would require a great amount of discipline related to all of the traits you'll discover in *Blue-Collar Leadership® & Teamwork*. But, my focus had to become very intentional in the area of developing myself and the rest of my large team (everybody at the facility) relative to learning about and applying Lean Manufacturing principles throughout the manufacturing and administrative processes.

I was committed to the leaders and the rest of the team, but to follow through on that commitment required me to "Be Intentional" like never before. I had to develop the discipline to read every day. I had no experience in leading Lean or in leading Lean teams. So, I leveraged the "Be Disciplined" trait and started reading Lean content daily for the next three years. If you have an interest in this area, be sure to check out my book, *Blue-Collar Kaizen: Leading Lean & Lean Teams*. It's not focused on improving the processes. It's focused on unleashing your team's potential.

Because everyone at the facility, including those on the small process improvement teams I was leading, knew I had no experience as a Lean Leader, I would have to be very intentional if I wanted to build trust with them during the process. I would have to be knowledgeable. But most importantly, we would have to get results together. And, we did.

We improved from -3% gross profit margin to +35% in three years. We accomplished amazing things together.

As you can guess, the low impact players didn't make it happen. They were focused, but they were focused on telling everyone why it wouldn't work, why it was a bad idea, and why we shouldn't be making changes to things that were working just fine and had "always been that way." If we had followed the advice of the low impact players, the facility would have been shutdown a few years later. Everyone would have lost their jobs.

The high impact players didn't buy what the low impact players were selling. Instead, we all became intentional and responsible for making it happen. As a result of their efforts, the plant became profitable, sales nearly doubled, and eventually the workforce grew by 10% with the addition of more team members.

When leaders become intentional about a new initiative such as Lean Manufacturing or Leadership Development, the great divide happens. I've witnessed this many times over the years in many different facilities with many different teams. The overall team divides into two teams. The positive, high impact players who support the leader's vision and mission and the negative, low impact players who are going to resist everything the high impact players choose to do in order to move the organization in the right direction.

When Blue-Collar Bob's leader asked him to be on the process improvement team and Bob committed, he was absolutely being positive, but he was also being responsible, flexible, and intentional. That small shift in Bob's mindset changed how he saw himself.

Bob chose to be on the team. When he did, he began to think like a high impact player. He went back to his work area with a focus on improvement. Before that, he had simply been going through the motions. But that day, he became intentional. He wanted to make a positive impact.

Bob started improving things on the spot without anyone telling him. He started moving things around in his work area to save time. Then, he began to notice it was actually easier to do his work. By the time the first team meeting happened, Bob had already increased his daily output by 10% without anyone's help or anyone's input. And, his job was easier, not harder.

Bob wondered, "What would happen to our team, company, city, country, and our world if everyone walked through the door every day to 'Be Intentional' about improving their jobs and their lives?" His mind raced to another quote he had seen on the board by Jim Rohn, "If you work hard on your job you can make a living, but if you work hard on yourself you can make a fortune."

*"I will never have all of the answers, but that will not stop me. I will go with what I have." ~ Jimmy Collins*

# TRAIT 10

## BE DRIVEN

### PURPOSE CREATES FOCUS

*"Success comes to those who hustle while they wait."*
*~ Thomas Edison*

High impact players are driven from the inside. Low impact players are driven from the outside. Inspiration is about what's happening within, on the inside of us. Motivation is about what's happening on the outside of us, what others are trying to get us to do.

My wife Ria is one of the most driven people I know. It's one of the many traits that make her a high impact player no matter what type of team she's on. She recently shared these words with her followers on social media, "I once thought you had to 'be somebody' to make a difference. A celebrity, a famous person, or Mother Teresa. But in truth, those who change the world start by changing themselves. You begin by becoming a person who CAN influence others in a positive way. And then, you become a person who is WILLING TO influence others in a positive way. You have the opportunity to make an impact and a difference right where you are. Doing so requires you to sacrifice - you must pay the price to improve yourself in order to become equipped to improve others. You cannot give others what you don't have. Becoming more valuable, so you can add value to others, is a responsibility you shouldn't take lightly. That's why I read 50 personal growth and leadership books every year - I'm working on developing myself, so I'm better equipped to help others. That's certainly not the only way to grow, but it's one way. And, it's the way that works well for me." Ria's words are strong. She is driven.

Ria doesn't have a blue-collar background, but that's what is so great about principles. They apply to everyone in every industry in every location. The timeless, tested, principles and traits high impact players embrace and align themselves with are always the same. What is different is the story about how and where they are applied and the stories about what others are able to accomplish with their teams. The principles are always the same; the stories are usually different.

In the blue-collar world, "Be Driven" can mean many things, but it always means you don't wait for someone to tell you what to do. You either do what you know should be done because it needs doing, or you seek out a leader and recommend to them what you believe should be done and get their approval or discuss an alternative task.

Low impact players make a habit of waiting to be told what to do. Their goal is often to do their eight and hit the gate. They think, "Why would I ever ask for something to do when I don't have anything to do?" I don't know about you, but that's not the mindset I want on my team. They are not driven, not taking responsibility, not focused, and most importantly, not going to get very far in life or very far up the pay scale.

High impact players are at the other end of the spectrum. They're already thinking about what to do next before they finish the task they're working on. They're likely to have a "To Do" list someplace. They're driven to make things happen and to make things better. That's the type of players I want on my team. How about you?

When I was on the front lines as an entry level worker, I accepted a job as a production cell operator which meant I was operating multiple machines by myself. There was a twin spindle lathe, a gear shaper, and a vertical milling center. I may have been working alone, but relative to the big picture, I was definitely part of a big team.

Why was I considered a high impact team player while I was working alone? Because I was driven to improve my piece of the organization. It's just who I was. No one taught me to do it, or trained me to do it, or shared a book like this with me. I was just naturally driven to be productive and to improve processes. I was on the team.

Without anyone telling me to do it, I created a log with all of the cycle times for each machine related to each part manufactured in the work cell. It took a while to record them all, but I did it one day at a time.

Then, I became intentional about looking for ways to shorten the cycle time on the slowest machine for each part. The first year, I helped double the output of the cell without anyone ever telling me to do it. That was a 100% increase in output. I did what I could and gathered up a support team (my supervisor, the machine programmers, the engineers, etc.) to help me when I needed them.

Not only was I able to produce twice as much, the operators on the other shifts could too. Of course, the low impact players were angry with us for "making them work harder." But, it wasn't harder. It was easier.

High impact players make it happen while low impact players ask themselves, "What happened?"

*"Success bases our worth on a comparison with others. Excellence gauges our value by measuring us against our own potential." ~ John Johnson*

# TRAIT 11

## BE INSPIRED

### GO WITHIN OR YOU WILL GO WITHOUT

*"I have never seen great performers who felt themselves to be out of control of their own performance, emotions, direction, purpose, decisions, beliefs, choices, or any other human faculties. They don't blame others or external factors. The greats are not like lesser performers, who try to explain away their failure as being somehow caused, forced, or controlled by someone else." ~ Henry Cloud*

To "Be Inspired" means you are driven from within. You are moving yourself forward. Motivation is about others trying to move you forward. Those "others" are often inspired from within unless their boss is motivating them to act. In that case, the boss is attempting to motivate someone who isn't inspired. Inspired players enjoy being motivated, but they don't require it to act. They're going to move themselves and the organization forward whether there's external motivation or not.

Let's use this book as an example.

If you purchased this book for yourself without someone telling you to purchase it and read it, then you were inspired from within. You didn't need someone motivating you to become a better team player. You're doing it on your own because you have an internal desire to get better. You're also more likely to help others get better, which will be external motivation for them.

However, if someone else purchased this book for you and asked you to read it or is leading you through a book study, that person is attempting to motivate you. They are likely hoping you become inspired and move beyond motivation.

You've made it to Trait 11. Are you motivated or inspired? How do you know? If you're continuing to read it because you are interested and want to read it, you have become inspired. If you're continuing to read it only because someone else wants you to read it, you're being motivated to read it. It's that simple. When we're doing something because we want to, we're inspired to do it. When we're doing something because someone else wants us to do it, we're being motivated to do it.

High impact players want to be better people, better teammates, and better at work. For them, getting better is not about making more money. It's about releasing the potential that lies within them. When they get better and do better, they feel better about themselves, and that's extremely rewarding to them. High impact players don't have to focus on the external motivator of money because it's not what drives them. However, they are likely to earn more money, promotions, and opportunities because they are inspired, positive, focused, flexible, responsible, and disciplined game changers.

Low impact players generally focus on making more money because for them the money is an external motivator. They may also want to get better, but it's so they can make more money. If they do more work than they are required to do or make improvements to their processes, they feel they are being used and abused if they're not rewarded because for them the reward must come from the outside. If they don't get the external reward, they often become negative.

High impact players are not average. They are exceptional sought after team members. High impact leaders are always searching for more high impact players to add to their team.

The key to moving beyond average and becoming exceptional is doing what high impact players do, not wanting what they have. It's easy to want what others have. However, it's much more difficult to do what they had to do to get what they have. Too often, low impact players feel threatened by the high impact players on their team. Instead of picking up their game and becoming a high impact player, low impact players often attempt to bring the high impact players down to their level.

I've had many low impact players try to bring me down to their level. In the late 1990's, I was operating a lathe and a drill press on the second shift. I had come in a few minutes early to speak with the first shift operator as I often did, so I'd be better prepared for the night ahead.

He looked a bit irritated as I walked up. He said, "Mack, why are you always trying to make us look bad?" I asked, "What do you mean?" I had no idea. He replied, "You run a lot more than 100% production. That makes us look bad because we're only doing the 100% that's expected." My production was usually 130%-150%.

I was blown away by his comment. I knew the first and third shift guys were low impact players. I also knew I wasn't making them look bad. They were making me look good. They could have done what I was doing, and I would have appeared average instead of exceptional.

*"The thing that makes us love our jobs is not the work that we're doing, it's the way we feel when we go there." ~ Simon Sinek*

# TRAIT 12

## BE PROUD

### EXHIBIT CONFIDENCE WITHOUT ARROGANCE

*"Often, the most difficult ego to deal with is your own."*
*~ Jocko Willink*

High impact players get results which means they also get attention. Because they consistently get results, they are very confident in their abilities. Or, because they are confident in their abilities, they get results. It's actually a combination of both.

It's important to apply Trait 3 "Be Humble" while you're being proud. High impact players are humble. Being humble doesn't mean you can't be proud of yourself and what you've accomplished. It does mean you avoid thinking how awesome you are because of it.

Norman Vincent Peale said it best, "Believe in yourself! Have faith in your abilities! Without a humble but reasonable confidence in your powers, you cannot be successful or happy." Take pride in who you are and what you've accomplished. "Be Proud." If being proud causes you problems, it's likely because of how you're being while you're being proud.

In my book, *Blue-Collar Leadership®: Leading from the Front Lines*, I shared this observation, "There's a fine line between arrogance and confidence. It's called humility. Confidence – Humility = Arrogance." The moment you show confidence without humility is the moment you've chosen to be arrogant. Arrogance is a choice to be cocky.

There's a big difference between being confident and being cocky. Confident teammates build trust. Cocky teammates create distrust. Simon Sinek got it right when he remarked, "Confidence is believing you're good. Cockiness is believing you're better than anyone else."

Confident players help and add value to their team. Cocky players devalue and hurt their team. High impact players are always confident but never cocky. They use their confidence to lift others to the next level and beyond. They humbly share their knowledge with others in an effort to help them become more confident.

It's important to know there are two basic types of confidence: self-confidence and situational-confidence. Ria explains this very well in the following five paragraphs which are an excerpt from her book, *Leadership Gems: 30 Characteristics of Very Successful Leaders:*

"Self-confidence is conviction of your values and core beliefs enhanced by experience and lessons learned from both successes and failures. In other words, self-confidence is static. The factors that make you uniquely you create your self-confidence. Self-confidence is developed over time. While other people can support you, self-confidence will only be realized by growing and developing your own character.

Situational-confidence is certainty in the outcome of a situation which is enhanced by your knowledge, skills, and abilities. In other words, situational-confidence is dynamic and is affected by factors outside of your control. Situational-confidence can be increased by developing your competency.

You won't always have situational-confidence. There will be times when you try something new, take on a new job, or first become a manager and lack experience or technical knowledge. There will be times when you have a new relationship with a team member and lack confidence in their ability to get the job done.

You may have self-confidence because it's based on your character which remains the same in every situation but lack situational-confidence. For example, you may lack situational-confidence, perhaps in a new job, and still have plenty of self-confidence in your ability to learn.

That shows strength of character because it takes self-confidence to develop situational-confidence. The more self-confidence you have (without arrogance), the greater success and influence you will have." ~ Ria Story

High impact players exhibit self-confidence in all situations. When it comes to situational-confidence, they know what they know and are secure enough to admit what they don't know. They don't pretend to know when they don't know. They will either seek out the knowledge to accomplish the mission themselves, or they will seek out someone on their team who has the knowledge and ability to help them accomplish the mission.

In the past, Blue-Collar Bob would get very defensive when someone questioned his knowledge, skills, or abilities. But, as he began to "Be Positive," he realized his defensive nature came across as being negative. In order to avoid being negative, he learned to simply admit what he didn't know and "Be Proud" about what he did know.

Bob noticed his new approach invited others to share their knowledge and to offer valuable feedback.

*"You will never get to the next level if you can't embrace feedback about your performance at the current level." ~ Henry Cloud*

# TRAIT 13

## BE BRAVE

### DO THE RIGHT THINGS
### FOR THE RIGHT REASONS

*"Having the moral willpower to put ethical principles
above self-interest and always do the right thing takes
a lot of character, especially when no one else seems
to be living up to such high standards."*
*~ Michael Josephson*

When I began to intentionally adopt the traits I'm sharing with you on these pages, "Be Brave" was the one that caught me by surprise. As a high impact player, I had to be courageous in ways I hadn't imagined before. I discovered I would need the courage to stand alone and lead, often without authority, as I adopted principles my teammates didn't value and didn't want to adopt. Being brave often means leading the way by being the first to change what needs to be changed.

As Blue-Collar Bob was heading out one Friday afternoon, he was approached by an excited teammate with a piece of paper in her hand. As she handed Bob the paper, she said, "Hi Bob! I've noticed you've taken an interest in the quotes posted on our bulletin board. Well, a friend of mine shared something interesting on social media recently, and I thought you might enjoy reading it. So, I printed off a copy for you."

Bob was surprised she had noticed his interest in the

quotes and even more surprised she had thought of him in this way. He was excited to see what she had brought. "Thank you very much Judy!" Bob replied, as she spun around and hurried toward her car and the weekend.

Eager to know what was on the page, Bob blocked out everything else as he began to slowly read the words, "Within every church, business, or nonprofit organization in need of change, there is a group of insiders who are keenly aware of the transformations that need to take place. They go home every night and gripe to their spouses. They gather in the break room and complain to each other. But day after day, they go about their work resigned to the notion that nothing will change. They are convinced that to try to introduce change would be a costly — and potentially hazardous — waste of time. So, they keep their mouth shut and watch the clock. They don't lack insight into what needs to happen; they simply lack the courage to do anything about it." ~ Andy Stanley

"Guilty as charged!" Bob thought to himself as he stared at the page. "But," he continued his thought, "I am improving. At least, I've stopped complaining." Then, he read it again realizing he, like many others, had been playing small. Bob read the quote many times over the weekend as he wondered to himself each time, "What can I do? What should I do? How can I do it? When will I do it? What's stopping me from doing it?"

After much thought, Bob determined fear was stopping him. He was afraid of what others would think and say if he took action. He had learned a lot as he had been intentionally applying the principles in the quotes he had been reading. Bob had already taken some heat from the teammates he was closest to. They said he was changing. They were right. He was.

Late Sunday evening, Bob decided he would go in on

Monday morning and share some of his ideas with his supervisor. "What will it hurt?" he thought to himself.

Monday afternoon finally arrived, and Bob's shift had ended. He headed out to his truck with an uneasy feeling inside. He had spoken with his supervisor several times, but he didn't have the courage to share a single idea. He had let himself down, and he knew it. He also knew he had let his team down because his ideas, if implemented, would help them too.

On Tuesday morning as Bob stood staring at the bulletin board, he felt like someone knew exactly what he needed to hear as he read the words by Melvin Maxwell, "Five frogs are sitting on a log. Four decide to jump off. How many are left?" Bob paused and answered to himself, "One because four jumped off." As he continued reading the rest of the quote, it was as if Maxwell had read his mind. "No, not one. Five. Why five and not one? Because there's a difference between deciding and doing!"

Bob quickly added the quote to his file and went to find his supervisor. The principle in the quote hit him hard. He had only decided to do something Sunday night. He hadn't actually done anything. He knew he had to move beyond deciding and start doing. "What a lesson!" he thought.

High impact players do more than decide to make a difference. They understand courage is a choice to do the right thing for the right reason at the right time. You may read this book and decide to do something different. But, you must act. You may have to lead when no one wants to follow. You will have to "Be Brave."

*"Every time I see someone that says,
'I have a weak leader,' I always say, 'Lucky you!'
Take advantage of that. LEAD!" ~ Jocko Willink*

# TRAIT 14

## BE TEACHABLE

### EMBRACE A BEGINNER'S MINDSET

*"The most fundamental success
factor is one's mindset." ~ Alan Weiss*

Being teachable means more than being willing to learn. To "Be Teachable" means you are willing to listen, learn, and seek knowledge from multiple sources. High impact players listen to teammates with the intention of learning from them regardless of their position, title, rank, or job description.

The key to being teachable is to be curious. Be curious about what your teammates know and their viewpoint. Each teammate knows something other teammates don't know. Those closest to a problem most often know the most about the problem and at a minimum can contribute valuable information to help solve the problem.

Low impact players rest on what was learned in the past, in college, at trade school, or their last job. They don't intentionally seek to learn more each day. High impact players believe they need a 50 year education (endless learning throughout their lives) to be successful and valuable. They remain teachable throughout their entire career and are constantly growing. They realize this: Learning more causes them to become aware of all the things they don't know. In other words, the more they know, the more they realize what they don't know.

Napoleon Hill shared these interesting thoughts in the early 1900's, and they still apply nearly 100 years later, "The average person who wanted to get an education would probably think first of some college or university, with the false belief that these institutions could 'educate' their students. But nothing in the world would be farther from the truth. The fact of the matter is that all any school on earth can do, save one, is to prepare a foundation for acquiring an education, and that one exception is the school of life, through the instruction books of human experience. Don't forget this. Don't believe for a moment that you can buy an education with money. You can't do it. An education is something you have to work for. Furthermore, it cannot be acquired in the usual four years given over to college training. If we are good students, we are going to school always. We never get through. Life is one continuous school, and the kind of students we are depends upon the kind of work we do as we go through this great university."

Being teachable requires you to leverage Trait 3 "Be Humble." You have likely already noticed Trait 3 is a key foundational trait that makes it possible for you to adopt and benefit from the application of many of the other traits. Without humility, becoming a high impact player isn't possible. Humility is one of the most important "Golden" traits.

Low impact players who are arrogant and ego-driven aren't teachable. Whether they know or whether they don't know, they want everyone to think they know. And, they won't slow down to listen to anyone who tries to share information with them. They think, "Why do I need to listen to someone explain something that I already know? It's a waste of my time." I'm sure Louis

Armstrong had low impact players with this type of mindset in mind when he remarked, "There are some people that if they don't know, you can't tell them."

There are two key reasons high impact players remain teachable:

1) Being teachable allows you to build relationships with your teammates. Listening, even when you really do know, always demonstrates respect for teammates and builds trust. Not listening when a teammate has something to share is disrespectful and always creates distrust.

2) Being teachable allows others to "Be Responsible." If you're allowing a teammate to teach you something, they become responsible for helping you succeed. Even if you know how to do something, being teachable allows you to help develop the confidence of a new teammate with no experience or a young teammate with little experience. Let them teach you as they're learning.

High impact players never forget: It's not about me, but it starts with me. Growing and developing their teammates is part of their personal mission. When they're being teachable, they are modeling humility and many other traits for teammates who may not have reached the high impact status and are still striving toward it.

High impact players know someone is always watching. The question is never, "Am I a role model?" But rather, "What kind of role model will I be?"

*"If we become increasingly humble about how little we know, we may be more eager to search."*
*~ Sir Ian Templeton*

# TRAIT 15

## BE OPEN-MINDED

### THERE'S ALWAYS ANOTHER WAY

*"We keep moving forward, opening new doors, and doing new things, because we are curious, and curiosity keeps leading us down new paths."*
~ Walt Disney

High impact players aren't always simply looking for a solution. They are focused on finding the best solution. They intentionally ask their teammates questions, not only to learn, but also to promote deeper thinking and shared ideas.

Low impact players compete with one another. Because they're *competing* instead of *completing*, they want to provide the solution in order to get the credit. As a result, they aren't open-minded when it comes to adopting ideas or accepting input from others. They are close-minded. They're afraid if another teammate gets the credit they won't get the credit.

High impact players complete one another. They don't focus on getting credit, although they are given a lot credit. Sometimes, they're given too much credit. Other times, they're given credit for things they didn't do. However, they don't seek credit. Due to their humility, even when they deserve the credit, they attempt to pass it on to their teammates.

As time passed, Blue-Collar Bob continued to make

improvements. When he looked in the mirror at himself, he felt good about the person he was becoming and the person he was leaving behind: the old, negative, unconcerned, and rigid Bob. He was making progress, building relationships, and expanding his influence.

Much to Bob's surprise, he was continuing to make great progress on his job too. He spent his days working hard. But because of the growth within him, he was also spending his days thinking about his job and how he could continue to make small and steady improvements. Bob was still a bit resistant to outside suggestions. At least, he was resistant in a positive way and resisted with a smile.

Bob strolled up to the bulletin board one morning with thoughts of how to make additional improvements to his work area on his mind. He started to think a little deeper as he began to read the newly posted quote with words by Woodrow Wilson, "I not only use all the brains I have but all that I can borrow." Bob thought that made a lot of sense as he thought to himself, "Who wouldn't use all the brains they could borrow? That's common sense. Anyone could and should do that."

As Bob made his way back to his work area, he was replaying the quote in his mind as he always did in an effort to memorize it before he arrived and got too busy with the work ahead.

Bob was able to remember the quote easily because it was short, had a flow to it, and was actually a bit humorous to him. But all of a sudden, it was as if someone had hit him over the head with a board as thoughts began to flood his mind, "This isn't what I do. Sure, I'm being positive, but I don't want anyone's ideas on how to improve my area. I reject the ideas of others with a smile and a 'Thanks, but no thanks.' I'm not using all the brains I can borrow. I've only been using mine. Why do I reject help from others?"

Bob made it to his area and got busy. But instead of diving into thoughts about improving the area, he spent the day in deep thought trying to figure himself out. "Why do I reject help? After all, isn't someone sharing an idea with me a form of help?"

As Bob continued to reflect, he kept arriving at the same question, "I know people are trying to help me. Why won't I accept it?"

As quitting time neared, he finally discovered the answer he had been searching for all day, "I'm close-minded! Close-minded people reject ideas from others. It's their way or no way. That's my problem!"

Bob immediately began to think about how negative he had been in the past when someone wanted to share an idea with him. Now, he was beginning to put the pieces of the puzzle together. One of the main reasons he had been negative was because he didn't like hearing others' ideas. Bob had learned being extremely negative, and sometimes even hateful and angry, toward others caused them to seldom share their ideas. He had turned being negative into a type of wall to keep others away.

"What a mistake!" Bob thought as all of the pieces fell into place. But then, a new thought rushed into his mind, "I stopped being negative, so that means I can stop being close-minded." He felt better. He began to imagine what would happen if he chose to "Be Open-Minded." He wondered, "How much better will my life be? How much better will my job be? How much more can I accomplish with my brain and 'all that I can borrow?'"

*"The successful man will profit from his mistakes and try again in a different way." ~ Dale Carnegie*

# TRAIT 16

## BE APPROACHABLE

### WHO YOU KNOW
### DETERMINES WHERE YOU GO

*"My success, personally and professionally, is based on my ability to connect and communicate. And, so is yours." ~ Ria Story*

You're now halfway through the 30 traits of high impact players. Pause for a moment. Look outward at everyone on your team. Imagine what it would be like if every team member in your company, onsite and offsite, including the front line workers and everyone on the support teams such as leadership at all levels, engineering, maintenance, warehousing, inventory control, shipping, receiving, quality, safety, IT, accounting, purchasing, sales, customer service, marketing, etc. were intentionally embracing, learning, and applying these traits.

Imagine if everyone was a high impact player.

What would be different? What would change within the organization? Would you have a better team? Would your company be a better place to work? Would you attract better teammates and be more likely to retain the high impact players already on the team? Would you feel better while at work? Would there be less stress?

I suspect it's pretty easy to look outward and ask "What if…?" while thinking of the low impact players on your team at all levels who really do need to change.

Those who, if only they would change, could make your day much better. Most likely, there are some who need to change in a big way. We all have room for improvement. No one is exempt when it comes to getting better. We can all get better. They can. I can. You can.

Now for the hard work. Look inward and ask yourself this question, "What if I intentionally chose to embrace, learn, and apply these traits?"

What would happen? Would you be doing your part as you expect everyone else to do their part? Would your influence increase? Would you develop more meaningful relationships? Would life at work be better? Would life at home be better? Would you be more valuable to your company? Other companies? Would you be more or less likely to be seen as promotable? Would you be seen as part of the problem or part of the solution?

Would you be more approachable? Would it matter?

We first make our choices, then our choices make us.

In my twenties, especially my early twenties, I wasn't an approachable person. I wasn't worried about teamwork. I was focused on my work and proving myself to the bosses. They talked about and hoped for teamwork. But, production is what they truly desired.

In those days, I proved myself by being the most productive person. I'm not happy to share that if someone asked me, "How do you produce so many parts on your shift?" Instead of sharing with them my methods, I was more likely to say, "I'm not going to tell you my secrets. You'll have to figure it out for yourself just like I did. No one told me. I'm not telling you." Or, I would simply say, "I work hard from the time I get here until the time I leave. You should try it sometime." I wasn't very approachable.

I'm proud to say I've come a long way since then. I've

achieved amazing transformation personally and professionally. My passion to help others climb to the next level and beyond comes from my transformation.

In my early career, I didn't know what I didn't know and no one was teaching me. There were plenty of bosses who were often telling me, sometimes demanding, that I should be a better team player. However, they were never teaching me or the rest of the team "how to be" better team players. Very few leaders were modeling the traits I'm sharing. Being given a position or title didn't transform leaders magically into high impact players. The leaders still didn't know what they didn't know.

I joined the U.S. Marine Corps as an infantryman right after high school in 1987. We were taught "how to be" a team and expected "to be" a team. But, in the civilian workplace, my leaders hoped and wished we would be a team. Hoping and wishing aren't strategies.

As a result of my USMC days, I carried a chip on my young shoulder. I even polished it every chance I got, so everyone could see it shine. I thought I was the man.

I simply wanted people to leave me alone and to stay away. Many in the civilian workforce had attitudes like mine, for various reasons, and were not approachable. Many of our leaders were not approachable. We were all on the same team, but we all shared a lot of the same weaknesses which made us low impact players.

To become more approachable, I started to adopt some of the traits I've shared already and some I'll be sharing later. They all add up in a big way. But ultimately, I had to start building relationships.

*"Relationships are about relating. If you don't spend time relating with your team, there won't be any relationship." ~ Rob Waldman*

# TRAIT 17

## BE HELPFUL

### WHAT YOU DO REVEALS WHO YOU ARE

*"We have to humble ourselves, and the way we do that is by serving other people." ~ Tim Tebow*

For me, this trait delivered results and brought me out of the shadows. When I chose to "Be Helpful," I was also choosing to intentionally build relationships. I didn't know about all the traits I'm sharing with you now. I simply stumbled my way forward as best I could through a lot of seemingly endless trial and error.

It's only when looking back across my 30 year, mostly blue-collar, career and with 10 years of reading leadership and personal growth books every day that I can reflect and see my mistakes and successes clearly. Without all of the growth from the many hundreds of books and many thousands of hours of audios and videos on various content like you're learning now, I wouldn't be able to turn the stories into meaningful lessons.

Fast forward 30 years, and I'm a high impact player who remains "under construction" because we never truly arrive. We're always traveling onward and upward if we're living on purpose for a purpose. Now, I'm living to grow and develop my teams, and there are many of them.

My journey to "Be Helpful" started on the front lines in a manufacturing factory 25 years ago. I wasn't very helpful beyond producing parts for the first five years of my 30 year career, so I'm not counting those as being very helpful to others. Today, my journey to "Be Helpful" that started 25 years ago has led me to a new team, a very big team, a team no one could have helped me imagine even 10 years ago. I couldn't see it.

I'm on your team because I want to "Be Helpful" to you. I'm also on the team of the many thousands of people around the world who read my books, watch my videos, and read my social media posts and blogs on LinkedIn and Facebook where Ria and I have nearly 75,000 combined followers as of mid 2018.

By becoming extremely intentional about applying what we were learning, we grew beyond the walls of the corporate jobs we held in really great companies. Our desire to help more and more people excel eventually caused us both to resign and rebuild our lives around helping people who value what we have to give.

Many people will incorrectly think we do what we do for the money. The money we generate is simply a byproduct of helping people across our nation and around the world. If you become intentional about building relationships purely to help people excel at work or at home, you are likely to generate that same byproduct because you will become more valuable to more people. Not because of what you may want now (more money), but because of what you may want to do going forward (help more people however you can wherever you can whenever you can because you can).

Where did we start? Right where we were when we chose to "Be Helpful." Who did we help? Anyone we could with what we had. There's always someone on your team who you can help. They may need your help at work, or they may need your help after work. They may need the knowledge you acquired last week or last year.

Each team member has a unique set of life experiences and work experiences waiting to be unleashed. Most people have no idea how valuable they are because they haven't learned how to leverage their value for their team. Many hold themselves and their teammates back. Many allow their teammates to hold them back.

Consider the impact of these words from Mark Twain, "Thousands of geniuses live and die undiscovered — either by themselves or by others." Don't choose to live and die undiscovered.

"Another day another quote," was running through Blue-Collar Bob's mind as he walked toward the bulletin board for his daily dose of personal motivation and inspiration. This had become a daily ritual, a habit, for Bob. On the weekends, he still had to have his morning boost. He started searching for quotes on the internet on his days off to fill the void. A small group had begun to gather around the board for their morning coffee to discuss the daily quote and what it meant to them.

As Bob approached to find out what wisdom the board would reveal, a small group had already formed. Little did Bob know, he was about to discover a life altering combination of words spoken by one of the greatest quarterbacks to ever lead a football team. He gazed up at Peyton Manning's words, "The most valuable player is the one that makes the most players valuable."

The words impacted Bob in a new and powerful way. They gave him a higher sense of purpose. He felt he should and could make a bigger difference. "What does it mean to you Bob?" someone asked. "Be Helpful," he replied. "I should be more helpful," he continued.

*"We all have the power to help many people, but do we have the courage to start with one?" ~ Tom Telesco*

# TRAIT 18

## BE OBSERVANT

### WITH PEOPLE, THE SMALL THINGS ARE THE BIG THINGS

*"People who are empathic are more attuned to the subtle social signals that indicate what others need or want." ~ Daniel Goleman*

The key to being helpful is to first "Be Observant." Pay attention to others, so you can be helpful when an opportunity appears. This means you must shift the focus from yourself to the team. It doesn't mean you don't take care of yourself and value yourself. You must absolutely focus on yourself. You can focus on your needs while maintaining an awareness of your team's needs. As Ken Blanchard stated, "People with humility don't think less of themselves. They just think about themselves less."

The Auburn University Equestrian Team's Head Coach, and the winner of five National Championships, Greg Williams is a personal friend of mine. He and his coaching staff were also clients of mine for several years. No one I know is as observant as Greg when it comes to being helpful. He has a sixth sense and instinctively knows when someone needs help.

However, it's really not a sixth sense. Greg is simply intentional about being observant and focused on those around him. For instance, if someone drops something and Greg is in the room, he's on his way to pick it up before it hits the floor. He's the first to open a door for someone or stay behind and hold the door for others who are entering or leaving.

Greg is quick to help because he has a heart to help. It's in his DNA. Being observant may not be in your DNA, but it can be learned. I've seen Greg in action at dinner parties in his home, in his office at Auburn University with his staff, and even on the mountain bike trails we built and rode together at Chewacla State Park in Auburn, Alabama.

In 2012, I volunteered to be the Founding President and Ria volunteered to be the Founding Secretary of the local mountain bike startup chapter, the Central Alabama Mountain Pedalers (CAMP). When I agreed to lead the team of volunteers who had asked me to be the Founding President, Greg was the first to volunteer to become a board member because he wanted to help me and the CAMP team revitalize the state park. In just a few months, we had over 150 volunteers on the CAMP team.

Ria and I served for nearly two years before we stepped aside. The plan from the start was to get it going, then hand it over to the Vice President, Philip Darden. Since being established in 2012, CAMP has accomplished amazing things and is still full speed ahead. From the very beginning, the CAMP motto was, "We make things happen!" We made things happen then, and they still do now. Over 30 miles of amazing mountain bike trails have been built, the majority by hand. Various racing events are held there annually. The park was struggling before CAMP organized. But now, park profits have skyrocketed as attendance has increased dramatically.

CAMP and the Chewacla State Park Staff are now recognized nationally for what they've accomplished together as hundreds of volunteers with a heart to help came together to accomplish some really great things.

Today, people travel from across the country to ride the nearly vertical 15' tall 'Great Wall of Chewacla', the 'Forbidden Zone' with more than 25 dirt jumps, and the endless miles of single track, cross-country trails throughout the park. Auburn High School formed a high school mountain bike team to compete across the state and recently won the State Championship.

What caused the amazing transformation of Chewacla State Park? Initially, it was a group of people who observed a need, chose to form a team, and made the decision to "Be Helpful." The park needed help far beyond what they could accomplish with their small paid staff. In the end, the park won, the mountain bikers won, the trail runners won, the hikers won, the community won, the state won, and the thousands of people from across the country who will improve their health on the trails for decades to come won and will continue to win.

In the words of Tim Sanders, "You don't help others because of who they are and how they can repay you. You should help them because it gives you an opportunity to do something incredible with all that you've learned and all you've become." How do you know what it is you need to do for others? First, you consider what physical and mental abilities you have within you that will benefit others. Then, you must "Be Observant" and look for opportunities where you can do things to add value to others using what you have within.

When you help your teammates, you build trust. If they need your help but don't get it, you create distrust.

*"A basic truth of life is that people will always move toward anyone who increases them and away from those who devalue them." ~ John C. Maxwell*

# TRAIT 19

## BE ENGAGED

### ENGAGEMENT LEADS TO INVOLVEMENT

*"I am responsible for taking action, asking questions, getting answers, and making decisions. I won't wait for someone to tell me. If I need to know, I'm responsible for asking. I have no right to be offended that I didn't 'get this sooner.' If I'm doing something others should know about, I'm responsible for telling them." ~ Garry Ridge*

High impact players are always engaged beyond what is required. They don't expect someone else to be responsible for their results. They take ownership of themselves and their team's results.

High impact players don't blame others for not telling them information they need to know. They are engaged and find out what they need to know. Instead of waiting for the information to find them, they find the information. On the other hand, if they have information others on their team need, they don't wait for them to ask for it. They intentionally make sure they provide it.

Imagine if all of your teammates at every level had this mindset and this level of engagement.

Low impact players are exactly the opposite. They are quick to blame a teammate for not providing the information they needed. Low impact players are quick to make excuses and slow to find a way to make things happen. They are also likely to have information teammates need but don't share it unless someone asks them for it. And sometimes, they don't share it then.

Listen to the voices of disengaged, low impact players:
- "That's not my job."
- "Sorry, I forgot to tell you."
- "That's above my pay grade."
- "I'm just here to get a check."
- "They don't pay me to think."
- "That's not my responsibility."
- "I didn't know. No one told me."
- "How is it my fault? I didn't know."
- "If they would have told me sooner…"
- "I'm here to do my eight and hit the gate."
- "You should have known I needed to know."

There's no doubt Napoleon Hill had low impact players in mind when he wrote the following words, "It is the practice of the majority of men to perform no more service than they feel they are being paid to perform. Fully eighty percent of all whom I have analyzed were suffering on account of this great mistake. You need have no fear of competition from the man who says, 'I'm not paid to do that, therefore I'll not do it.' He will never be a dangerous competitor for your job."

A common phrase I've heard shared among the blue-collar workforce is, "I'm just here to get a check." I have never understood the mindset of someone who will openly admit to their teammates they are happy to sit on the bench and watch everyone else do the work of moving the team and the organization forward.

These low impact players are actually advertising to

anyone who will listen that they are disengaged. The disengaged aren't likely to be promoted, given raises, or given new opportunities to excel. I've also listened to these same low impact players blame everyone else but themselves for having been in the same position since they were hired. I saw that as an amazing accomplishment. I couldn't believe they still had a job.

Blue-Collar Bob wanted to be more engaged and received permission to post quotes on the bulletin board every other week. It was Monday. He was posting his first quote, one from Billy Taylor that had really caught his attention, "In the absence of ownership comes blame."

"Ain't that the truth," thought Bob. He had witnessed it in his own life, in the mirror to be more precise. When he was traveling down Negative Street, he was focused on blame. Personal ownership was nowhere in sight. He was blaming everyone for everything, and he truly believed whatever was wrong in his life, at work or at home, was someone else's fault.

But, that was in the past. Bob had become engaged and had taken a sharp, sudden right turn onto Positive Street, and things looked a lot different there. He had stopped blaming others, not to intentionally become engaged, but rather to "Be Positive."

Becoming engaged was a byproduct of being positive.

While Bob was blaming others, he didn't feel he had to do anything. When he stopped blaming others and started taking ownership, he felt he had to do everything. He realized, "The moment I take responsibility for everything is the moment I can start changing anything."

*"Being proactive will allow you to stand out among your peers as someone who is a leader or who has leadership potential." ~ Ria Story*

# TRAIT 20

## BE PRESENT

### MINE THE GOLDEN NUGGETS; DUMP THE DIRT

*"If I read a book that cost me $20 and I get one good idea, I've gotten one of the greatest bargains of all time." ~ Tom Peters*

High impact players never lose track of their personal mission: growth and development. To become highly successful, they know they must become highly valuable. Therefore, they do everything with purpose. They walk with purpose. They talk with purpose. They work with purpose. They live with purpose. When it comes to life, they are fully present.

Ria and I speak at various blue-collar organizations all across the United States. We have spoken to teams maintaining ships for the U. S. Navy in San Diego, California, teams in the Public Works Department in a large county government near Washington D. C., teams pumping concrete in Charlotte, North Carolina, teams installing fireplaces and garage doors in Grand Prairie, Texas, and to many more teams making things happen in their own industries.

One message I often share with these teams is, "Mine the golden nuggets; dump the dirt." What I mean is to "Be Present." If you're reading a quote, reading a book, listening to an audio, watching a video, or listening to someone speak at a conference or in your break room, always look for the golden nuggets. They are everywhere. Sometimes, you will find many of them. Sometimes, you may only find a few of them.

Real miners who are mining for actual gold dig up much more dirt than gold. Does that cause them to stop mining? Absolutely not. They mine the gold and dump the dirt continuously, endlessly seeking what they value: the gold.

High impact players are similar to miners. They are both looking for what they value and ignoring the things they don't. High impact players seek wisdom and knowledge from many sources in many places. If they're reading a book or listening to someone speak, they're searching for the golden nuggets which are thought provoking phrases or ideas that catch their attention. And, they dump the dirt which is everything else.

Low impact players are not interested in mining for golden nuggets. First of all, you won't find them reading books or participating in any form of personal development. Second of all, they will moan, groan, and whine when they're challenged to learn something new at work. They are resting on their schooling and not interested in a lifetime of education. When they're in a meeting or training, they're not really there. Their body may be, but their mind is not. They're much more likely to be scrolling mindlessly on their phone than seeking to capture a great thought or idea in their notes.

In my continuing education, I mined a single golden nugget that allowed me to transform my life. In 2008, I was exposed to personal development content for the first time in the form of a 1-hour audio a friend had given me in 2005. Don't miss that. It took me three years before I chose to listen to it. But when I did, everything began to change, much like Blue-Collar Bob's life began to change when he discovered the golden nuggets of wisdom on the bulletin board for the first time.

For me, it was a 1-hour audio summary of *The 7 Habits of Highly Effective People* written by Stephen R. Covey. Within the first few minutes, Covey shared a thought and planted the seed of transformation within me. He said, "Between stimulus and response, we have the freedom to pause and choose our response." I had never considered what I had just heard for the first time. My short temper was all the evidence you would have needed to confirm that truth. I seldom paused and chose my response. I most often reacted instantly based on my emotions.

I'm happy to report I was present that day. I no longer have a problem with my temper. I now pause and choose a response that doesn't include anger. I mined the golden nugget that day in 2008.

When Blue-Collar Bob started checking the bulletin board, he unknowingly had started mining golden nuggets. He was learning to "Be Present." Someone on his team had first mined the golden nuggets. Then, they did more than required. They started sharing what they were learning with their team. Bob had started doing the same. Leadership is influence, and Bob was leading.

It was Tuesday morning. Bob was posting his second quote of the week. He was sharing the following golden nugget he had mined from William A. Ward, "Study while others are sleeping; work while others are loafing; prepare while others are playing; dream while others are wishing." Mining this nugget the previous Saturday at 6:00 am, Bob had begun to study while others were sleeping.

*"Know how to listen and you will profit even from those who talk badly." ~ Plutarch*

# TRAIT 21

## BE UNDERSTANDING

### SEEK TO UNDERSTAND WHAT OTHERS ARE SEEING AND FEELING

*"Empathy, another ability that builds on emotional self-awareness, is the fundamental 'people skill.'"*
~ *Daniel Goleman*

There's a difference between sympathy and empathy. The Merriam-Webster online dictionary states, "The difference in meaning is usually explained with some variation of the following: sympathy is when you share the feelings of another; empathy is when you understand the feelings of another but do not necessarily share them."

High impact players seek to understand others. Understanding a teammate is much different than agreeing or disagreeing with a teammate. Teammates who aren't normally listened to often mistake another's understanding as agreement. When you are seeking to understand others, be sure to declare your intent up front to avoid a misunderstanding.

High impact players communicate clearly, "I'm not here to agree or disagree. I simply want to make sure I understand how you see things and why you see things the way you do." This sets the stage for high impact communication. To truly move beyond communication to connection while trying to understand, learn to squint with your ears and listen with your eyes. To better understand, listen and look for meaning between words.

The easiest way to influence a teammate is to allow them to first influence you. When you choose to allow others to go first, to allow them to be understood first, you're choosing to transfer influence to them. Your actions and maybe even your words are literally communicating, "I'm willing to wait. I'm willing to be sure I understand you before I expect you to attempt to understand me." This is a powerful high impact trait. Transferring influence allows you to gain influence.

When a teammate feels understood, they are mentally prepared and ready to listen to what you have to say because they have confirmed it is based on a full and complete understanding of their position. However, if you try to get others to understand you first, they're usually not listening at all because they're not sure you fully understand. If they think you don't understand, their focus is not on listening but on helping you understand. In other words, they are more concerned with talking than listening.

High impact players want to be understood when they communicate. They don't want to waste their time talking to someone who isn't listening. As they seek to understand, they reflect the other's feelings by describing their emotions with words such as, "I can see you're upset." Or, "I sense you want to say more." Or, "I can tell you would rather not talk about this now."

High impact players also rephrase content to help others feel understood. When they're having a high stakes conversation with a teammate where emotions are high, high impact players replay what they are hearing with phrases that start with, "Let me repeat what I think I just heard you say..." Or, "To make sure I understand you clearly, allow me to repeat back what I heard..." Or, "I heard you say..., but I'm sensing you also feel..."

Low impact players focus all of their energy on being understood. They want to go first. It's easy to tell when they don't feel understood. They get louder, more animated, and become frustrated. If everyone involved in the conversation is a low impact player, no one is seeking to understand first. Although everyone is talking, no one will be heard. We may decide when we will speak, but others decide if they will listen.

It was Wednesday, Blue-Collar Bob's third day of posting quotes. He had a quote to reinforce the wisdom from Mark Twain about "schooling and education" which he had discovered on the board weeks earlier. Bob mined this nugget from Aristotle, "Educating the mind without educating the heart is no education at all."

Bob reflected back on his schooling realizing all of it had focused on his mind. He began to understand it was his heart that was holding him back the most, not his mind. He didn't feel guilty because he didn't know what he didn't know. However, now he knew.

Bob was beginning to realize it was his character, his "heart," that would launch him to the next level, not his competency, his "mind." For Bob, it was all starting to come together as he thought, "Before I can understand others well, I first must understand myself well. Understanding others may be the easy part, but understanding myself will likely be the hard part." Bob was looking forward to continuing his education.

*"When we listen deeply to the other person, we are listening to the words they say and the words they don't say. We are listening to the feelings they are expressing." ~ Ria Story*

# TRAIT 22

# BE COMPETENT

## LEVERAGE STRENGTHS;
## IGNORE WEAKNESSES

*"Making strengths productive is much more than an essential of effectiveness. It is a moral imperative. To focus on weakness is not only foolish; it is irresponsible." ~ Peter Drucker*

The principle in the quote above is absolutely powerful and true. However, context is key to fully understanding and mining the golden nugget which it contains. "To focus on weakness is not only foolish; it is irresponsible." This nugget <u>only</u> applies in the area of competency. It <u>does</u> <u>not</u> <u>apply</u> in the area of character.

Understanding this principle is critical for high impact players who want to maximize and leverage their competency.

When it comes to competency, you will excel and become a highly valuable asset to your team when you focus on intentionally developing and maximizing your strengths. Your strengths are strengths because you're naturally good in those areas with little effort. With average focus, you will remain average. With intense focus, you will become exceptional. High impact leaders highly value exceptional team members.

When it comes to competency, you can't excel and you won't become highly valuable to your team if you focus on developing your weaknesses. You can absolutely become more valuable, but you won't become highly valuable. Your weaknesses are weaknesses because you're not naturally good in those areas. Even with above average focus, you will remain average at best. Leaders appreciate average team members, but they are not as highly valued as exceptional team members.

High impact players know they should work on both strengths and weaknesses. They also know these two secrets to success: 1) In areas of character, work to improve your *weaknesses* because they will hold you in place like an anchor; and 2) In areas of competency, work to improve your *strengths* because they will launch you like a rocket.

Focus on these two secrets at the same time, and you'll launch to the next level and beyond faster than you could have ever imagined. You will become a highly valued and highly sought after team member with many options.

*Blue-Collar Leadership® & Teamwork* is packed full of principles that will help high impact players, and those who want to become high impact players, improve and develop the character traits that low impact players don't value. Character is responsible for 87% of your results and influence, but you still must develop your strengths relative to competency in order to excel.

Your character will determine if your team wants to work with you and accept your influence. Your character will allow you to build mutually beneficial relationships. However, it's your competency that will allow you to contribute to the organization's mission. When there's a unifying purpose, a shared vision, and a shared mission, your competency will allow you to convert your character-based relationships into meaningful results and success for the team and the organization.

Character + (the appropriate) Competency = Trust

Without a high degree of character, all the competency in the world is of little use because few people want to work with low impact teammates who have poor character. However, I'm sure you're aware of people who work on mediocre teams with teammates who have poor character. It happens all the time. But why?

Typically, people are willing to work with low impact players for one of two reasons: 1) They don't have options, so they "have to" work with them; or 2) They have shared values, so they "want to" work with them.

High impact players have many options. One option is not to work with low impact players and teams. You won't find the highest impact players on a low impact team unless there is a reason. The #1 reason is because they are helping transform the low impact team into a high impact team. It takes a high degree of character and competency to transform a low impact team into a high impact team. It can only be done by high impact players.

Blue-Collar Bob was at the board on Thursday with powerfully inspiring words to post from James Allen, "Let a man radically alter his thoughts, and he will be astonished at the rapid transformation it will effect in the material conditions of his life." Bob thought silently, "When I started intentionally changing my thoughts, my thoughts started automatically changing my life."

*"It's not more knowledge, it's not more education we need, and it's not more facts. It's a better use of what we already have that we need to have."*
*~ Napoleon Hill*

# TRAIT 23

## BE CERTAIN

### DO YOU KNOW?
### OR, DO YOU THINK YOU KNOW?

*"Don't speak with certainty on an issue of which
you are unsure!"* ~ *John C. Maxwell*

In all of my 30 plus years working in and supporting
the blue-collar workforce, one of the things that most
amazed me was the "rumor mill" or the "grapevine." It
was always churning with unverified facts shared by the
uninformed as facts. Misinformation was transferred
from the bottom to the top, from the top to the bottom,
from left to right, and from right to left. I discovered
rumors can travel in any direction at any speed.

Various team members at all levels were subject to be
spreading rumors in an effort to be seen as "in the loop"
or "in the know" to gain credibility and recognition.
However, they often lost credibility because they didn't
actually know but wanted to appear as if they did. Team
members who didn't know but thought they knew were
constantly spreading misinformation.

They may have received their information from
someone they believed should have actually known.
Then, they spread it as fact because they believed their
source was reliable. I've learned over the years the rumor
mill isn't something that only occurs on the front lines
where information tends to be scarce. It occurs at every

level of the organization because team members at all levels, all the way to the very top, are subject to say things they believe to be true but don't know to be true.

When you say something you believe is true but don't know with 100% certainty to be true, you've shared a guess not a fact. High impact players avoid spreading a guess as a fact because they place a high value on integrity and credibility. When you spread guesses instead of facts, you risk damaging your credibility and integrity.

One of the great traits high impact players exhibit is to "Be Certain" before they speak. One of the most important lessons I learned early on while leading process improvement teams in manufacturing plants was the importance of adopting the trait of being certain.

When I started leading process improvement teams, I didn't know what I didn't know. I would trust those on the team who were supposed to know. I learned very quickly to slow down and verify. When someone would speak what they believed to be fact, I learned to ask, "Do you know? Or, do you think you know?"

If they hesitated before answering, I assumed they were trying to determine if they knew or if they thought they knew. If they said "I know" instantly, I assumed they thought they knew, but I also assumed they still may not know. With or without a hesitation to answer, I asked an important follow up question if they answered "I know." I would ask, "How do you know?" This is when I and the rest of the team would discover the trail we were about to travel in order to "Be Certain."

Andy Stanley made a great point about leadership when he remarked, "Saying 'I don't know' when you don't know is a sign of good leadership. Pretending to know when you don't is a sign of insecurity. By expressing your lack of uncertainty, you give the leaders around you permission to do the same thing. You send them an important message: In this organization, it is okay not to know. It is not okay to pretend you know when you don't." Remember, leadership is influence. Stanley's words apply to anyone with a desire to be a high impact player regardless of position, title, or rank.

High impact players are secure within. They will quickly say they don't know when they don't know. Low impact players are on the other end of the spectrum. They tend to be insecure and much more likely to say they know when they don't know.

"Be Certain" to build trust with your teammates. Track down the truth before you spread the rumor, not after. Your credibility and integrity are on the line with every word you speak.

Blue-Collar Bob was a bit more excited than usual as he approached the bulletin board on Friday morning to post his fifth quote of the week. This one was by Weston H. Agor, "Intuition is what we know for sure without knowing for certain."

Bob was excited because of the discussion he expected to hear around the board. He had saved this quote until Friday because he thought it was a bit deeper than usual which meant a deeper discussion with varying opinions. By posting this quote on Friday, his team would have the entire weekend to think about it before receiving their next golden nugget the following Monday.

In the past, Bob had shared thoughts based on intuition with others as fact. He thought he knew "for sure," but he didn't know "for certain." Going forward he wanted to also "Be Certain" before sharing his thoughts.

*"Your pride will blind you to what you most need to learn." ~ Paul Akers*

# TRAIT 24

## BE MOTIVATIONAL

### MOTIVATION LEADS TO INSPIRATION

*"Logic helps people to think,*
*but emotion urges them to act." ~ Alan Weiss*

Low impact players tend to manipulate their teammates for their own benefit. Manipulation is influencing teammates to act for your personal gain. Manipulation creates distrust among the team. Manipulation destroys relationships. Manipulation stimulates the wrong emotions within your teammates.

High impact players motivate their teammates by seeking mutual benefit. Motivation is influencing teammates to act in a way that allows everyone to win. Motivation builds trust among your team. Motivation strengthens your relationships. Motivation stimulates the right emotions within your teammates.

Motivation requires an external source. Something outside of you causes you to act. When you take action to help your team win because an external source has influenced you, you have been motivated. When you take action to help your team win without external motivation, you are inspired from within.

High impact players are able to motivate others because they have experienced being motivated by others. Motivation causes teammates to act when you're in their presence because of your presence.

When I was leading teams focused on 5S activities (Sort, Shine, Set in order, Standardize, & Sustain), it often included cleaning very dirty, oily industrial equipment that may not have been cleaned in 10 or even 20 years. I would find the dirtiest piece of equipment in the target area. Then, I would help my team members clean it. I didn't have to. I wanted to because I wanted to be on the team. I wanted to "Be Motivational."

As an outside consultant serving as their team leader, I knew it would be hard for other team members to complain about the task if I was engaged and helping on the dirtiest part of the project. When I led teams, I was never just the team leader although that was also my responsibility. I was always a part of the team. When I'm on a team, I want to be a high impact player who is helping make things happen.

Motivating the team is a responsibility that high impact players embrace. By helping tackle the dirtiest piece of equipment at the very beginning, I began to build influence and motivate the rest of the team. Because I was there, engaged with them, helping them, appreciating them, they were motivated to act.

Most of these events were 5 Day events. Because we were motivated, we were also having fun while performing a hot, dirty, yet rewarding job. The teams were proud of their successes and the results we achieved together. On Fridays, they were always excited to present their before and after pictures to the leadership team and tell the story of all we had accomplished together. I made it a practice to stand in the back of the room. It wasn't about me. It was about the team. I didn't want any credit because they deserved all of the credit.

I've also witnessed low impact team leaders attempt to

manipulate their teams. Most often, these team leaders had a position of authority within the organization and used it to direct the team instead of using their character to motivate the team. The result: a mediocre event with poor results and frustrated team members.

Those who manipulate others will demoralize them. Those who motivate others are likely to inspire them.

High impact players with positions of authority don't use their formal authority to direct their team. They set it aside and use moral authority to motivate their team. The foundation for moral authority is character. Team members without formal authority don't have a choice. They must learn to motivate and influence their teammates with character in order to become a highly effective high impact player.

After a week of posting quotes, Blue-Collar Bob was looking forward to once again being surprised as he made his way to the bulletin board Monday morning. The board revealed a powerful golden nugget from the legendary Green Bay Packers Coach Vince Lombardi, "Coaches that can outline plays on a blackboard are a dime a dozen, but the ones that can succeed are the ones that can get inside their players and motivate them."

Bob was the first to arrive at the board which gave him a head start on gathering his thoughts for the group discussion. A fellow "gold miner" arrived soon enough and stared at the board in silence. "So, what do you think about this one Bob?" he asked. Bob was ready with his answer, "I think Lombardi was doing far more than just coaching his team from the sidelines. I think he was on the field within each player helping execute the plays."

*"Lead and people will follow;*
*point and people will run." ~ Paul Akers*

# TRAIT 25

## BE INSPIRATIONAL

### INSPIRATION LEADS TO ADMIRATION

*"There is always a choice about the way you do your work, even if there is not a choice about the work itself." ~ Lundin, Paul, & Christensen*

Those who are motivated often become inspired. High impact players are not only motivational team members. They are also inspirational team members. Their influence stretches far beyond their presence.

I was in a manufacturing facility near Dallas, TX in 2010. I was there "training the trainers." Two team members of the onsite Lean Team within the facility were co-leading a 5 Day TPM (Total Productive Maintenance) event where a large roll former was being rebuilt in place on the plant floor by the assembled team. It was a large and aggressive project that required a large and motivated team in order to accomplish the mission.

It was the type of event I really enjoyed leading. However, I wasn't officially leading it. I was simply there to support those who were leading the event as they began to do what I had previously been doing, leading process improvement teams. The two team leaders were learning, growing, and taking more ownership which had been the goal from the start.

Most of Day 1 was classroom instruction and discussion. Day 2 was when the real action would start.

On Day 1, I was mostly observing. The two team leaders were well prepared, sharp, and well respected. If they had questions, I was happy to assist. Assisting usually meant asking them a question that would lead them to their own answer. By asking questions, they discovered they already had the answers within. They just didn't always realize it.

By the end of Day 1, the team had an action plan for Day 2. They would be focused on disassembling the large, dirty machine down to the frame. There would be a lot of parts to remove, clean, and track during the disassembly process. Then, the entire frame which was nearly 25' long, 6' wide, and 3' tall would need to be thoroughly cleaned before painting and rebuilding could start on Day 3.

On Day 2, I wandered in and out of the area to monitor the team's progress. Although I wasn't officially leading the event, I was officially responsible for the success of the event.

The two team leaders had participated on many events with me in the past when I was leading, and they were learning. I knew they were motivated because they were making things happen. I wouldn't know if they were inspired until I saw them in action on their own. How would they perform? I found out late on Day 2 while checking on the team's progress.

I walked into the area to see how things were going. The team had made amazing progress. All 10 team members were hot and filthy. The machine was a skeleton of what it had been that morning. As planned, nothing remained but the frame.

The last task for the day was to clean the frame. That's what the team was doing when I arrived. I noticed the two team leaders were underneath the frame cleaning. Thanks to a team member who was pressure washing the top side of the frame above them, they were covered in water, oil, and grease like everyone else. When the two team leaders saw me in the area, they made their way out to tell me about the team's many accomplishments.

I was on the team but in the shadows. I had no worries. The two team leaders were high impact players. They would have succeeded if I had never shown up because they no longer needed to be motivated. They had become inspired and were learning to "Be Inspirational."

I was highly impressed by the team's results. But, I was more impressed by the two team leaders. They were inspired to "Be Motivational." They were doing the dirty work to motivate their team into action. They were covered from head to toe with oily water and grease. It was in their hair too! What made their example so powerful? These two team leaders were women!

They were definitely high impact players who desired to "Be Inspirational." Based on their team's performance, it was obvious their team admired them.

Blue-Collar Bob looked forward to coming to work every day now. He entered the door excited and ready to mine some gold. The latest nugget was from George Washington Carver, "When you do the common things in life in an uncommon way, you will command the attention of the world."

Bob felt proud as he let Carver's words sink in. He was a common man doing common things. But, he was starting to do them in an uncommon way, and "the world" was beginning to notice.

*"The needs of large-scale organizations have to be satisfied by common people achieving uncommon performance." ~ Peter Drucker*

# TRAIT 26

## BE AWARE

### UNTIL YOU'RE AWARE, YOU CAN'T BEWARE

*"All lasting growth requires awareness. Unfortunately, if you lack awareness, then you don't know that you are unaware. It's a blind spot. You don't know what you don't know, and you can't see that you are unable to see." ~ John C. Maxwell*

Something that separates high impact players from low impact players is their level of awareness. When it comes to awareness, the one thing you need to know about becoming a high impact player is there are many things you need to know about becoming a high impact player.

*Blue-Collar Leadership® & Teamwork* only begins to scratch the surface. There are all types of personal development books focusing on specific areas to help you raise your awareness. If this is your first book on teamwork, be aware because there are many more, and they all contain golden nuggets of wisdom. And yes, they all contain some dirt too. Remember, "Mine the golden nuggets; dump the dirt."

If you've enjoyed the style and content of this book, Ria and I have published more than 20 books to help you climb higher and higher up the mountain of awareness. You can learn more about them by visiting my website at BlueCollarLeadership.com/store or by searching for them on Amazon. They are also listed in the back of this book.

All are paperback and eBook. Many are also available on audio through Audible and Amazon.

If this book has raised your awareness, you must understand every book you read will likely raise your awareness in some area. It's one of the reasons I have been reading daily since 2008 and will continue until I die. I have blind spots just like everyone else, and I'm choosing to be intentional about overcoming them. But, we must also realize some will always be there.

High impact players know they have blind spots. They also know the biggest blind spot they have is most often located between them and the mirror. Therefore, they are actively growing and developing themselves while continuing to ask for feedback from their teammates.

An interesting thing about high impact players is their ability to be focused on their team's mission while being aware of the team's role in achieving the overall objective of the organization. Robert Rabbin put it this way, "Keep one degree of focus while maintaining 360 degrees of awareness. It means we pay total attention to what is right in front of us, without losing awareness of all that is around us." That's the goal: focus and awareness.

Because high impact players are constantly raising their level of awareness, they are positioned to raise the awareness of those around them. These sought after team players are easily motivated by other high impact players, and they are inspired to grow and develop their teammates without needing instruction or guidance from their leaders. Growing the team is their personal mission.

They are aware of the big picture and where they best fit. They know their passion and purpose better than anyone, and they leverage it to benefit their team, most often without recognition, behind the scenes in small but effective ways. It's who they are and what they do.

As you continue your upward climb and your awareness increases, don't beat yourself up over your past. It's common to learn something new and begin to see things in your past differently and with greater focus. It's also common to start looking in the mirror thinking about what you "should have done" or "could have done." Don't dwell on the past. Reflect on the past, capture the lesson, and use it to move forward more effectively into the future. As James Thurber remarked, "Let us not look back in anger, or forward in fear, but around in awareness."

Blue-Collar Bob had been reflecting a lot. As his awareness continued to increase, he began to view his past and himself differently. He was also beginning to look in the mirror much more, around his blind spot, in an attempt to see what kind of person he was becoming.

Bob had noticed nearly every quote posted on the bulletin board seemed as if it was meant specifically for him. This was simply because he was being intentional about looking in the mirror. The latest post credited to The Arbinger Institute was no different. The words hit hard as he began to read them, "No matter what we're doing on the outside, people respond primarily to how we're feeling about them on the inside."

This one stung Bob a bit. He had made a lot of progress, but he had become aware that much of it was on the surface. A thought quickly formed in Bob's mind, "I've been changing what I've been doing, but I must change how I'm being. I don't need to only do better. I need to be better."

*"You can't make the other fellow feel important in your presence if you secretly feel that he is a nobody."*
*~ Les Giblin*

# TRAIT 27

## BE CAREFUL

### SOME WILL LIFT YOU UP;
### SOME WILL TEAR YOU DOWN

*"If man chooses irrational values, he switches his emotional mechanism from the role of his guardian to the role of his destroyer." ~ Ayn Rand*

As a high impact player, you will absolutely have values that are much different from the average players and the low impact players on your team.

In a positive manner, your values are going to separate you from the pack. You will choose to lead teammates when necessary, and you will choose to follow teammates when necessary. High impact players are always in control of themselves and their future. As a result, you will have options that people of lesser character will not have.

Toxic teammates with a low degree of character and with values that conflict with yours are much more likely to try and bring you down to their level rather than choose to join you at a higher level. These toxic teammates attempt to contaminate the team, often with great success.

When low impact players see one of their own trying to rise to a higher level of effectiveness, they often use their influence to attempt to pull their teammate back down. I know because it's happened to me throughout my career as I continued to climb higher and higher.

When I first began to stop being a reactive, negative front line team member, much like Blue-Collar Bob was when I introduced him to you, I started building positive relationships with high impact players, my boss, and other leaders. As soon as my low impact teammates realized what was happening, they didn't congratulate me. They started doing what they do. They started accusing me of brown-nosing, sucking up, and much worse.

Those were the tactics of toxic, low impact players attempting to manipulate and shame me into remaining at their level. They were toxic because they were bad for me and my future. They had no desire to climb higher which was their choice. But, they also didn't want me to climb higher. Ultimately, that was my choice.

High impact players are able to control their relationships with toxic people. Because they have self-control and a high degree of character, they are able to interact with their toxic teammates without being negatively influenced by them. They are also strong enough to know when and how to end a relationship with a toxic teammate or even a toxic boss or employer.

High impact players are always in control and know how to avoid being controlled.

One of the greatest responsibilities of high impact players is to go back down the mountain to help others break free from those who are attempting to hold them back. They choose to build a relationship with those lower down the mountain in order to increase their influence with them. And hopefully, influence them to grow in a positive way.

I'm proud to say I had the courage to stand alone as I continued my climb and left the toxic players behind. Too many don't have the strength to make it out of the gravitational pull of toxic relationships, especially when there are no high impact players to help them transition to the next level and beyond. Often, it becomes easier for them to give in to the pressure and let others dictate their journey.

I'm reminded of one of my favorite quotes by James Allen, "We are anxious to improve our circumstances but unwilling to improve ourselves. We therefore remain bound."

I wrote *Blue-Collar Leadership® & Teamwork* to help you climb to the next level. As you do, "Be Careful" because there are many who won't support you. And, "Be Helpful" because there will be many who need your support during their journey.

Blue-Collar Bob was struggling. He was feeling torn. Some teammates were proud of his progress and others he had considered friends were giving him a hard time. He was starting to wonder if they really were his friends as he read the daily quote from Mahatma Gandhi, "The moment there is suspicion about a person's motives, everything he does becomes tainted."

"That's it!" Bob thought to himself. "Their motives have tainted our relationships. Why aren't they proud of me? Why are they trying to hold me back?"

Questions filled Bob's mind for the rest of the day. His teammates were losing his trust because they weren't helping him. And, some of them were even trying to hold him back.

*"It's the relationships we build and the people whom we trust that give us the courage to take risks and make ourselves better." ~ Rob Waldman*

# TRAIT 28

## BE OPTIMISTIC

### HOPE ISN'T A STRATEGY,
### BUT IT'S NEEDED TO DEVELOP ONE

*"People who are optimistic see a failure as due to
something that can be changed so that they can
succeed next time around, while pessimists take the
blame for failure, ascribing it to some lasting
characteristic they are helpless to change."*
~ *Daniel Goleman*

Those who are optimistic believe tomorrow can be
better. They believe they can be better. They believe their
teammates can be better. They believe their organization
can be better. They have a preferred vision for the future.

High impact players intentionally seek to turn their
vision into their reality. They're not just along for the bus
ride. They load their team on the bus and hop in the
driver's seat. Because they believe they can make things
happen, they find a way to make things happen.

As you become more focused on the traits of high
impact players, you must understand hope is a great thing.
However, hope alone won't take you and your team to
the next level. But, hope will help you get to the next
level. Hope begins with a vision of what could be.

Therefore, vision is the foundation of hope. Before a
person can have hope, they must first have a vision of
something better in their future. If the vision is clear, it

will produce hope.

Hope serves as the foundation for sacrifice. When you have hope, you're likely to begin making the needed sacrifices to turn your vision into your reality. Then, you must develop the discipline to leverage those sacrifices.

For instance, high impact players grow and develop high impact teams. You may be reading this book and thinking everyone on your team would benefit from reading it. The benefit you see is your hope and vision for a better future. But, hoping people will read this book won't cause them to read it. You must take action.

That action means you must make one or more sacrifices in order to turn your vision into a reality. At a minimum, you will have to sacrifice time. Then, you must have the discipline to schedule and conduct a meeting with your leader, if you aren't the ultimate decision maker, or with your team if you are. You may be asked to lead a book study or to contact me to become certified to teach this content. Someone will have to pay for the training resources. Whatever the price, it must be paid before your vision is turned into your reality.

Regardless of what you want to accomplish at home or at work, vision creates hope. Hope leads to sacrifice. Sacrifice is leveraged with discipline. And, discipline produces results.

The higher you climb, the harder it is to continue climbing. However, the higher you climb the greater your influence will be in all directions. It will likely get tough at times. "Be Optimistic" and keep climbing. Your team needs you at the next level. You may want to give up. Don't. You may want to slip back. Don't.

Blue-Collar Bob was still struggling with leaving his "friends" who were also his teammates behind. He didn't think he was better than them, but he did think he was becoming different than them. He still had hope he could influence them to climb higher up the mountain with him. He didn't want to leave them behind, but he wasn't staying behind. He was determined to move forward.

Some of Bob's teammates weren't buying what he was selling. They were doing what most people do when change happens. They were watching and waiting. They hadn't seen a reason to buy-in to Bob's vision yet. But, they knew one thing. Bob's discovery of the quotes on the bulletin board had changed him. He wasn't the same old Bob any longer. The old Bob had moved out.

Bob had been searching the internet for something to give him hope as he struggled to "Be Optimistic."

His search produced a short poem that inspired him to stay the course. It was titled *Thinking* by Walter D. Wintle, "If you think you are beaten, you are. If you think you dare not, you don't. If you like to win but you think you can't, it is almost certain you won't. If you think you'll lose, you've lost. For out of the world, we find success begins with a fellow's will. It's all in the state of mind. If you think you're outclassed, you are. You've got to think high to rise. You've got to be sure of yourself before you can ever win a prize. Life's battles don't always go to the stronger or faster man. But sooner or later, the man who wins is the man who thinks he can."

Bob had a thought, "There's hope for me, and there's hope for my team. I won't give in, and I won't give up."

*"Most people will achieve their greatest success one step beyond what looked like their greatest failure."*
*~ Brian Tracy*

# TRAIT 29

## BE REALISTIC

### YOUR VALUES ARE THE FOUNDATION OF YOUR CIRCUMSTANCES

*"Values are not simply posters on a wall. In order for a culture to be strong, your values must be clear and your values must be lived." ~ Simon Sinek*

The difference between high impact players and low impact players is the way they think. How you think is determined by what you value. When it comes to team building, dramatically different values always lead to dramatically different results.

For instance, some hope and wish their team would get better. But, that's about as far as they're willing to go toward making it happen. Why? Because they don't value responsibility, sacrifice, engagement, and discipline. Those values, plus others, are required in order to actually make a team better. High impact players share these values. Low impact players don't.

Any member on any team who is willing to pay the price of developing themselves can move their team forward. I've seen welders on the front lines do it. I've seen supervisors on the front lines do it. I've seen engineers do it. I've seen managers do it. I've seen the leaders at the top do it.

Influence is available to anyone who has the courage and determination to claim it.

Developing authentic influence is about earning respect. In my book, *Blue-Collar Leadership® & Supervision*, I wrote, "There is a difference between someone respecting your position and someone respecting you." Teammates with shared values will always respect you. Teammates who don't share your values may respect your position on the team, but they won't respect you.

As Lieutenant General George Flynn said, "Culture equals values plus behavior." If you want to change the culture of your team or throughout your entire organization, you must "Be Realistic."

The reality: You can't change the culture of the team without changing the values of the team. Why? Because the values of the team determine the behavior of the team.

As Blue-Collar Bob discovered, you can't make your teammates change their values. You can only attempt to influence them to choose to change their values. Your ability to influence others to embrace your values will be based on your ability to adopt and model those values.

We each choose our values. Your future begins with your values which fuel your thoughts which produce your feelings which influence your choices (actions) which lead to your results which determine your circumstances.

Your values form the foundation of your thoughts. For example, if you value developing yourself, you will think about how you could and should do it. If you don't value developing yourself, you won't have any related thoughts. What you value determines what you think.

Your thoughts form the foundation for your feelings. The thoughts you have create emotions within you. These feelings influence your choices. If you want to change your feelings, you must change your thoughts. What you think determines how you feel.

Your feelings form the foundation for your choices. Thoughts can be influenced by others. So, indirectly your feelings can be influenced by others. Your feelings never determine your choices, but they will always influence your choices. How you feel influences what you do.

Your choices form the foundation for your results. Every choice you make will produce a result. If you want dramatically different results, you must make dramatically different choices. You first make your choices; then your choices make you.

Your results form the foundation for your circumstances. When you add up all of your results, they equal your circumstances. As you've just learned, to change your circumstances, you must change your values. Your values are the root cause of your circumstances.

Blue-Collar Bob once again found himself in a deep discussion with the morning coffee crew at the bulletin board. Dov Seidman's words were being debated, "A handful of shared values is worth more than 1,000 rules."

If there was one thing Bob didn't like, it was rules. Someone asked, "Why do we have so many rules anyway?" Bob had begun to figure this one out a bit, so he was quick to answer, "Because we don't know how to behave. Each of us comes to work and behaves based on our individual values. We wouldn't need any rules if we had a set of shared values and chose to align our behavior with those values." Someone was quick to follow up, "How do we do that? Who decides what our team should value?" Bob was ready for that one too, "I believe the person posting these quotes is attempting to do that in a small way. But, we need to start asking around."

*"Aspiring to greatness is easy, achieving it isn't."*
*~ Ria Story*

# TRAIT 30

## BE RELENTLESS

### UNTIL YOU QUIT, YOU HAVEN'T FAILED

*"If we succeed, it will not be because of what we have, but it will be because of what we are; not because of what we own, but rather because of what we believe."*
*~ Lyndon B. Johnson*

As you strive to climb to the next level and beyond, your goal shouldn't be to be better than everyone on your team. Depending on your team, being the best may be easy, or it could be extremely difficult. Your goal should be to relentlessly help everyone on your team get better. To do that, you must continue to get better yourself. Your team is counting on you to be relentless.

You already know your teammates aren't living up to their full potential, neither are you. Neither am I.

It will always be easy to find people who haven't made it to your level yet. But, don't inflate your success by comparing how you're doing to how those who are behind you on the climb are doing. They aren't your competition. Neither are those who are ahead of you.

If you desire to be a high impact player, there's only two people you should compare yourself to: the one you were yesterday and the one you're capable of becoming tomorrow.

Comparing yourself to who you were yesterday allows you to see if you're doing something each day to intentionally get better, especially in the area of character. This is why I read either personal growth or leadership development books daily. Doing so allows me to say with integrity, "Yes, I'm doing something everyday to get better." My daily reading also keeps me fully aware of how far I have to go.

Comparing yourself to who you could become tomorrow if you were living up to your full potential allows you to evaluate how far you still have to go. That's one comparison that will provide any humble person with a reality check. That comparison will always reveal plenty of room for improvement.

As you strive to improve, don't allow the fear of failure to hold you back. What most people refer to as failure is actually learning. Think about this. Do we say infants are failing to walk or learning to walk? We say they're learning to walk because we know what the outcome will be. They won't fail to walk although they appear to be failing continuously. They will learn to walk.

After only a few months of life, infants can teach us lesson after valuable lesson about how to "Be Relentless." They continuously pursue their goals and never give up.

You only truly fail when you give up and quit trying. As Eric Greitens stated, "You will fail, especially in the beginning. And that's not just OK, it's essential. Without resilience, the first failure is also the last — because it's final. Those who are excellent at their work have learned to comfortably coexist with failure. The excellent fail more often than the mediocre. They begin more. They attempt more. They attack more. Mastery lives quietly atop a mountain of mistakes."

As you attempt to unleash not only your potential, but also your team's potential, you must "Be Relentless."

No matter how great you are, you can always get

better. Are you willing to be relentless in your pursuit to make more of an impact than you're making today?

It was Friday morning. Blue-Collar Bob was a little more excited than normal. He would be taking off at noon to start a long planned week of vacation at the beach. It had been his week to post quotes on the bulletin board. He had saved a special quote by Kyle Rote Jr., "There is no doubt in my mind that there are many ways to be a winner, but there is really only one way to be a loser and that is to fail and not look beyond the failure."

Unknowingly, Bob was becoming a high impact player. No one had ever talked to him about what type of player he was or wasn't. All he knew was his transformation had been very hard, sometimes nearly impossible. He had considered going back to his old, negative ways more than a few times when his boss or some of his teammates had rubbed him the wrong way. But, he didn't. Bob thought to himself as he walked away from the board, "Until I quit trying to be better, I haven't failed to be better."

*"It's always too soon to quit, and it's always easier to succeed at what you've started than to quit early and fail." ~ Truett Cathy*

I welcome hearing how this book has influenced the way you think, the way you lead, or the results you have achieved because of what you've learned in it. Please feel free to share your thoughts with me by email at:

Mack@MackStory.com

To learn more about my books, audio books, podcast, etc., please visit: BlueCollarLeadership.com

# ABOUT THE AUTHOR

Mack's story is an amazing journey of personal and professional growth. He married Ria in 2001. He has one son, Eric, born in 1991.

After graduating high school in 1987, Mack joined the United States Marine Corps Reserve as an 0311 infantryman. Soon after, he began his 20 plus year manufacturing career. Graduating with highest honors, he earned an Executive Bachelor of Business Administration degree from Faulkner University.

Mack began his career in manufacturing in 1988 on the front lines of a large production machine shop. He eventually grew himself into upper management and found his niche in lean manufacturing and along with it, developed his passion for leadership. In 2008, he launched his own Lean Manufacturing and Leadership Development firm.

From 2005-2012, Mack led leaders and their cross-functional teams through more than 11,000 hours of process improvement, organizational change, and cultural transformation. Ria joined Mack full-time in late 2013.

In 2013, they worked with John C. Maxwell as part of an international training event focused on the Cultural Transformation in Guatemala where over 20,000 leaders were trained. They also shared the stage with internationally recognized motivational speaker Les Brown in 2014.

Mack and Ria have published 30+ books on personal growth and leadership development. In 2018, they were invited to speak at Yale University's School of Management. They also had over 80,000 international followers at the end of 2019 on LinkedIn where they provide daily motivational, inspirational, and leadership content to people around the world.

Mack and Ria inspire people everywhere through their example of achievement, growth, and personal development.

Clients: ATD (Association for Talent Development), Auburn University, Chevron, Chick-fil-A, Kimberly Clark, Koch Industries, Southern Company, and the U.S. Military.

BlueCollarLeadership.com

## WHAT WE OFFER:

- ✓ Keynote Speaking: Conferences, Seminars, Onsite
- ✓ Workshops: Onsite/Offsite Half/Full/Multi Day
- ✓ Leadership Development Support: Leadership, Teamwork, Personal Growth, Organizational Change, Planning, Executing, Trust, Cultural Transformation, Communication, Time Management, Selling with Character, Resilience, & Relationship Building
- ✓ Blue-Collar Leadership® Development
- ✓ Corporate Retreats
- ✓ Women's Retreat (with Ria Story)
- ✓ Limited one-on-one coaching/mentoring
- ✓ On-site Lean Leadership Certification
- ✓ Lean Leader Leadership Development
- ✓ Become licensed to teach our content

## FOR MORE INFORMATION PLEASE VISIT:

BlueCollarLeadership.com
RiaStory.com
TopStoryLeadership.com

## FOLLOW US ON SOCIAL MEDIA:

LinkedIn.com/in/MackStory
Facebook.com/Mack.Story

LinkedIn.com/in/RiaStory
Facebook.com/Ria.Story

## LISTEN/SUBSCRIBE TO OUR PODCASTS AT:

TopStoryLeadership.com/podcast

Excerpt from

## *Defining Influence:*
### *Increasing Your Influence Increases Your Options*

In *Defining Influence*, I outline the foundational leadership principles and lessons we must learn in order to develop our character in a way that allows us to increase our influence with others. I also share many of my personal stories revealing how I got it wrong many times in the past and how I grew from front-line factory worker to become a Motivational Leadership Speaker.

# INTRODUCTION

### When You Increase Your Influence, You Increase Your Options.

*"Leadership is influence. Nothing more. Nothing less. Everything rises and falls on leadership." ~ John C. Maxwell*

Everyone is born a leader. However, everyone is not born a high impact leader.

I haven't always believed everyone is a leader. You may or may not at this point. That's okay. There is a lot to learn about leadership.

At this very moment, you may already be thinking to yourself, *"I'm not a leader."* My goal is to help you understand why everyone is a leader and to help you develop a deeper understanding of the principles of leadership and influence.

Developing a deep understanding of leadership has changed my life for the better. It has also changed the lives of my family members, friends, associates, and clients. My intention is to help you improve not only your life, but also the lives of those around you.

Until I became a student of leadership in 2008 which eventually led me to become a John Maxwell Certified Leadership Coach, Trainer, and Speaker in 2012, I did not understand leadership or realize everyone can benefit from learning the related principles.

In the past, I thought leadership was a term associated with being the boss and having formal authority over others. Those people are definitely leaders. But, I had been missing something. All of the other seven billion people on the planet are leaders too.

I say everyone is born a leader because I agree with John Maxwell, *"Leadership is Influence. Nothing more. Nothing less."* Everyone has influence. It's a fact. Therefore, everyone is a leader.

No matter your age, gender, religion, race, nationality, location, or position, everyone has influence. Whether you want to be a leader or not, you are. After reading this book, I hope you do not question whether or not you are a leader. However, I do hope you question what type of leader you are and what you need to do to increase your influence.

Everyone does not have authority, but everyone does have influence. There are plenty of examples in the world of people without authority leading people through influence alone. Actually, every one of us is an example. We have already done it. We know it is true. This principle is self-evident which means it contains its own evidence and does not need to be demonstrated or explained; it is obvious to everyone: we all have influence with others.

As I mentioned, the question to ask yourself is not, *"Am I a leader?"* The question to ask yourself is, *"What type of leader am I?"* The answer: whatever kind you choose to be. Choosing not to be a leader is not an option. As long as you live, you will have influence. You are a leader.

You started influencing your parents before you were actually born. You may have influence after your death. How? Thomas Edison still influences the world every time a light is turned on, you may do things in your life to influence others long after you're gone. Or, you may pass away with few people noticing. It depends on the choices you make.

Even when you're alone, you have influence.

The most important person you will ever influence is yourself. The degree to which you influence yourself determines the level of influence you ultimately have with others. Typically, when we are talking about leading ourselves, the word most commonly used to describe self-leadership is discipline which can be defined as giving yourself a command and following through with it. We must practice discipline daily to increase our influence with others.

*"We must all suffer one of two things: the pain of discipline or the pain of regret or disappointment." ~ Jim Rohn*

As I define leadership as influence, keep in mind the words leadership and influence can be interchanged anytime and anywhere. They are one and the same. Throughout this book, I'll help you remember by placing one of the words in parentheses next to the other occasionally as a reminder. They are synonyms. When you read one, think of the other.

Everything rises and falls on influence (leadership). When you share what you're learning, clearly define leadership as influence for others. They need to understand the context of what you are teaching and understand they *are* leaders (people with influence) too. If you truly want to learn and apply leadership principles, you must start teaching this material to others within 24-48 hours of learning it yourself.

You will learn the foundational principles of leadership (influence) which will help you understand the importance of the following five questions. You will be able to take effective action by growing yourself and possibly others to a higher level of leadership (influence). Everything you ever achieve, internally and externally, will be a direct result of your influence.

1. ***Why*** **do we influence?** – Our character determines *why* we influence. Who we are on the inside is what matters. Do we manipulate or motivate? It's all about our intent.

2. ***How*** **do we influence?** – Our character, combined with our competency, determines *how* we influence. Who we are and what we know combine to create our unique style of influence which determines our methods of influence.

3. ***Where*** **do we influence?** – Our passion and purpose determine *where* we have the greatest influence. What motivates and inspires us gives us the energy and authenticity to motivate and inspire others.

4. ***Who*** **do we influence?** – We influence those *who* buy-in to us. Only those valuing and seeking what we value and seek will volunteer to follow us. They give us or deny us permission to influence them based on how well we have developed our character and competency.

5. *When* **do we influence?** – We influence others *when* they want our influence. We choose when others influence us. Everyone else has the same choice. They decide when to accept or reject our influence.

The first three questions are about the choices we make as we lead (influence) ourselves and others. The last two questions deal more with the choices others will make as they decide first, *if* they will follow us, and second, *when* they will follow us. They will base their choices on *who we are* and *what we know*.

Asking these questions is important. Knowing the answers is more important. But, taking action based on the answers is most important. Cumulatively, the answers to these questions determine our leadership style and our level of influence (leadership).

On a scale of 1-10, your influence can be very low level (1) to very high level (10). But make no mistake, you *are* a leader. You *are* always on the scale. There is a positive and negative scale too. The higher on the scale you are the more effective you are. You will be at different levels with different people at different times depending on many different variables.

Someone thinking they are not a leader or someone that doesn't want to be a leader is still a leader. They will simply remain a low impact leader with low level influence getting low level results. They will likely spend much time frustrated with many areas of their life. Although they could influence a change, they choose instead to be primarily influenced by others.

What separates high impact leaders from low impact leaders? There are many things, but two primary differences are:

1) High impact leaders accept more responsibility in all areas of their lives while low impact leaders tend to blame others and transfer responsibility more often.

2) High impact leaders have more positive influence while low impact leaders tend to have more negative influence.

My passion has led me to grow into my purpose which is to help others increase their influence personally and professionally while setting and reaching their goals. I am very passionate and have great conviction. I have realized many benefits by getting better results in all areas of my life. I have improved relationships with my family members, my friends, my associates, my peers, and my clients. I have witnessed people within these same groups embrace leadership principles and reap the same benefits.

The degree to which I *live* what I teach determines my effectiveness. My goal is to learn it, live it, and *then* teach it. I had major internal struggles as I grew my way to where I am. I'm a long way from perfect, so I seek daily improvement. Too often, I see people teaching leadership but not living what they're teaching. If I teach it, I live it.

My goal is to be a better leader tomorrow than I am today. I simply must get out of my own way and lead. I must lead me effectively before I can lead others effectively, not only with acquired knowledge, but also with experience from applying and living the principles.

I'll be transparent with personal stories to help you see how I have applied leadership principles by sharing: How I've struggled. How I've learned. How I've sacrificed. And, how I've succeeded.

Go beyond highlighting or underlining key points. Take the time to write down your thoughts related to the principle. Write down what you want to change. Write down how you can apply the principle in your life. You may want to consider getting a journal to fully capture your thoughts as you progress through the chapters. What you are thinking as you read is often much more important than what you're reading.

Most importantly, do not focus your thoughts on others. Yes, they need it too. We all need it. I need it. You need it. However, if you focus outside of yourself, you are missing the very point. Your influence comes from within. Your influence rises and falls based on your choices. You have untapped and unlimited potential waiting to be released. Only you can release it.

*You,* like everyone else, were born a leader. Now, let's take a leadership journey together.

(If you enjoyed this Introduction to *Defining Influence*, it is available in paperback, audio, and as an eBook on Amazon.com)

Excerpt from

# 10 Values of High Impact Leaders

Our values are the foundation upon which we build our character. I'll be sharing 10 values high impact leaders work to master because they know these values will have a tremendous impact on their ability to lead others well. You may be thinking, *"Aren't there more than 10 leadership values?"* Absolutely! They seem to be endless. And, they are all important. These are simply 10 key values which I have chosen to highlight.

Since leadership is very dynamic and complex, the more values you have been able to internalize and utilize synergistically together, the more effective you will be. The more influence you will have.

*"High performing organizations that continuously invest in leadership development are now defining new 21st century leadership models to deal with today's gaps in their leadership pipelines and the new global business environment. These people-focused organizations have generated nearly 60% improved business growth, reported a 66% improvement in bench strength, and showed a 62% improvement in employee retention. And, our research shows that it is not enough to just spend money on leadership training, but rather to follow specific practices that drive accelerated business results." ~ Josh Bersin*

**Do you want to become a high impact leader?**

I believe everyone is a leader, but they are leading at different levels.

I believe everyone can and should lead from *where they are.*

I believe everyone can and should make a high impact.

I believe growth doesn't just happen; we must make it happen.

I believe before you will invest in yourself you must first believe in yourself.

I believe leaders must believe in their team before they will invest in their team.

I truly believe *everything rises and falls on influence.*

There is a story of a tourist who paused for a rest in a small town in the mountains. He went over to an old man sitting on a bench in front of the only store in town and inquired, *"Friend, can you tell me something this town is noted for?"*

*"Well,"* replied the old man, *"I don't rightly know except it's the starting point to the world. You can start here and go anywhere you want."* [1]

That's a great little story. We are all at *"the starting point"* to the world, and we *"can start here and go anywhere we want."* We can expand our influence 360° in all directions by starting in the center with ourselves.

Consider the following illustration. Imagine you are standing in the center. You can make a high impact. However, it will not happen by accident. You must become intentional. You must live with purpose while focusing on your performance as you develop your potential.

*Note: Illustration and 10 Values are listed on the following pages.*

**Why** we do what we do is about our *purpose.*

**How** we do what we do is about our *performance.*

**What** we do will determine our *potential.*

Where these three components overlap, you will achieve a
**HIGH IMPACT**.

## *10 Values of High Impact Leaders*

# 1

## THE VALUE OF VISION
### *Vision is the foundation of hope.*
*"When there's hope in the future, there's power in the present." ~ Les Brown*

# 2

## THE VALUE OF MODELING
### *Someone is always watching you.*
*"Who we are on the inside is what people see on the outside." ~ Mack Story*

# 3

## THE VALUE OF RESPONSIBILITY
### *When we take responsibility, we take control.*
*"What is common sense is not always common practice." ~ Stephen R. Covey*

# 4

## THE VALUE OF TIMING
### *It matters when you do what you do.*
*"It's about doing the right thing for the right reason at the right time." ~ Mack Story*

# 5

## THE VALUE OF RESPECT
### *To be respected, we must be respectful.*
*"Go See, ask why, and show respect"*
*~ Jim Womack*

# 6

## THE VALUE OF EMPOWERMENT
### *Leaders gain influence by giving it to others.*
*"Leadership is not reserved for leaders."*
*~ Marcus Buckingham*

# 7

## THE VALUE OF DELEGATION
### *We should lead with questions instead of directions.*
*"Delegation 101: Delegating 'what to do,' makes you responsible. Delegating 'what to accomplish,' allows others to become responsible."*
*~ Mack Story*

# 8

## THE VALUE OF MULTIPLICATION
### *None of us is as influential as all of us.*
*"To add growth, lead followers. To multiply, lead leaders." ~ John C. Maxwell*

# 9

## THE VALUE OF RESULTS
*Leaders like to make things happen.*
*"Most people fail in the getting started."*
*~ Maureen Falcone*

# 10

## THE VALUE OF SIGNIFICANCE
*Are you going to settle for success?*
*"Significance is a choice that only*
*successful people can make."*
*~ Mack Story*

Excerpt (Chapter 3 of 30) from
*Blue-Collar Leadership® & Culture:*
*The 5 Components for Building High Performance Teams*

# THE IMPACT OF CULTURE

## THOSE WHO WORK THERE WILL DETERMINE WHO WANTS TO WORK THERE

*"I think the most important and difficult thing is to create a culture in the organization where leadership is really important. It's important for people in the company to realize that this is a growth-oriented company, and the biggest thing we have to grow here is you, because it's you who will make this company better by your own growth. ~ Jim Blanchard*

Listen to the voices of leaders who are losing the labor war:

- "We just can't find any good people."
    As if…there aren't any good or great people.
- "Due to the low unemployment rate, there just aren't any good people left."
    As if…the only people who can be offered a job are those without a job.
- "In today's labor market, those who want to work are already working."
    As if…those who are working at one place can't decide to work at a different place.
- "When we do get good people, they won't stay."
    As if…the problem is always with the people and never with their leaders.

One thing I know about leaders who make these and similar comments is this: Their culture is a competitive disadvantage. Someone else has the advantage and is winning the battle for the good and great people. The good and great people certainly aren't out of work wishing they had a job. They're working someplace else.

Until a leader is aware of the problem, they can't address the problem. In case it's not obvious, the problem is their culture. The leader owns this problem whether they want to or not. Every time I hear these comments, and I hear them a lot, I know I'm talking to a leader who doesn't know what they don't know.

Ria and I hear leaders across varying blue-collar and white-collar industries repeatedly making these comments as we travel across the USA speaking on leadership development. These voices seem to be getting louder and louder. In fact, these voices are an inspiration for this book.

There are many leaders in blue-collar industries needing help. I want to help them stop searching for good people and start attracting great people. The transformation won't happen overnight. However, until it starts happening, it's not going to happen. My intention is to use this book to raise awareness while providing a transformational road map for those leaders who want to make their culture their greatest competitive advantage.

We were speaking in Louisville, KY recently to owners of blue-collar organizations. Afterward, one approached and said, "There isn't a magic pill is there? I think we all hoped there was." I replied, "No sir. There isn't a magic pill or an easy button. This is how you build a high performance team and an exceptional culture that will attract, retain, and support them. There is no other way."

Your culture is always attracting certain types of people and repelling others. Who we are is who we attract. This principle applies to individuals as well as organizations. The culture within your organization is negatively or positively impacting those within the organization, and some who are outside the organization.

The key point is to understand the people inside your organization are constantly providing the most influential type of advertising about your organization and the leaders within it. It's called word of mouth advertising. How your team is feeling inside the organization will determine what they're saying outside the organization.

If what they're saying about their leaders and the organization to others is good, it'll be easier to find good people. If what they're saying is great, it'll be easier to attract great people. But, if what they're saying is bad, finding good people will be hard, if not impossible.

Remember the voices at the start of this chapter? Those leaders had team members who were sharing bad word of mouth advertising about the organization. Unless those leaders choose to change, nothing will change.

Common sense reveals it's easier to win the labor war while attracting great people instead of searching for good people. However, what's common sense isn't always common practice. Often, it takes uncommon sense to act on things that are commonly understood. Creating an organizational culture that will attract and retain great people requires leaders with uncommon sense.

The best led companies aren't impacted by labor shortages because they're consistently attracting the best and the brightest people to their organizations.

*"If we lose sight of people, we lose sight of the very purpose of leadership." ~ Tony Dungy*

Excerpt (Ch. 5 of 30) from
*Blue-Collar Leadership®:*
*Leading from the Front Lines*

# THERE IS AN "I" IN TEAM

## EVERY TEAM IS MADE OF "I"NDIVIDUALS

*"I'm just a plowhand from Arkansas, but I have learned
how to hold a team together – how to lift some men up, how
to calm others down, until finally they've got one heartbeat
together as a team. There's always just three things I say:
'If anything goes bad, I did it. If anything goes semi-good,
then we did it. If anything goes real good, they did it.' That's
all it takes to get people to win." ~ Paul "Bear" Bryant*

Paul *"Bear"* Bryant was one of the greatest college football
coaches to ever lead a team of young men down the field. He
was also a *"plowhand"* from Arkansas. A blue-collar worker. The
blue-collar world has produced some of the greatest leaders of
all time, so you should be proud and hold your head high.
*Without them, the world as we know it would not exist.*

There's nothing holding you back but you. As my blue-
collar friend, Donovan Weldon, stated so well, *"The only person
between you and success is you. MOVE! The only person between you
and failure is you. STAND FIRM!"* Those are strong words of
wisdom. Donovan started on the bottom just like you and me.
But today, he's the CEO of Donovan Industrial Service in
Orange, TX near Beaumont.

Donovan's success didn't happen by accident. He made it
happen. You can make things happen too! He's a blue-collar
leader that believes in and develops his team on a regular basis.
I know because my wife, Ria, and I had the privilege of being
brought in to speak to his team about leadership in 2014. They
are making it happen on purpose for a purpose!

It's time for you to stop playing small and start playing tall.

A college degree is not required for you to play at a higher level. Not having one is simply an excuse some people use to continue playing small. If you want a college degree, use what you will learn on these pages to find a way to get one. If you don't want a college degree, use what you learn on these pages to make it happen without one.

You are the key to your success. You must believe in yourself. You must grow and develop yourself, which is what you're doing as you read this book. Do not stop growing! And when the time is right, you must bet on yourself.

Understanding your role as a team member is another must. Those on the front lines often underestimate themselves because they can't see the big picture. They can't see the value they have to offer. Far too often, their boss isn't a high impact leader and needs a lot of growth and development too. Bosses are often given the title without any formal development.

When I write about the front lines on these pages, I'm not only talking about the people in entry level positions. They are obviously on the front lines, but they also have leaders that are on the front lines with them and various team members supporting them too. They can all learn from these pages.

This book was written specifically for anyone at any level that visits, interacts with, or works on the front lines.

The principles I share with you must be applied if you want to make a high impact and be recognized for leading from the front lines. Regardless of your position, the more you apply these principles, the more options you will have, and the more positions you will be offered as you climb even higher.

Teams are made up of "I"ndividuals, so there are many I's on every team, regardless of how many times you hear, *"There is no 'I' in TEAM."* As a matter of fact, *you are one of them.* Every person on a team is an "I" and has the potential to lead (influence) the team, positively or negatively.

*"Leadership is influence. Nothing more. Nothing less."*
*~ John C. Maxwell*

You must understand there are many official and unofficial teams in the organization where you work. They are very dynamic and constantly changing.

When most of us think of which team we are on, we immediately think of our peers, the ones on the same crew, in the same department, or working on the same job. This is our core team, but it only represents the smallest team we're on. We also support other teams too, as others support our team.

When we choose to contribute beyond our immediate team, we are choosing to be part of a bigger team. Often, this only requires a choice to do so. Your choice to get involved in other areas sends a clear message to the high impact leaders.

When you play tall, you choose to contribute because you know it will increase your influence and your impact on the front lines. If you want to play tall, you should want to be noticed, to be selected, to volunteer, to share information, to accept more responsibility, and ultimately, to make a contribution at a higher level.

As a direct result of your choice to step up, your influence increases. You're demonstrating you can lead from the front lines and will be seen and respected by all high impact leaders as a high impact leader. Your actions will not go unnoticed.

When you play small, you choose not to contribute because you don't want to do more. If your goal is to coast until pay day, it won't be a secret you can keep. When you make every effort not to be noticed, not to be selected, not to volunteer, not to share information, not to accept responsibility, and ultimately to not contribute, *you will absolutely be noticed*.

As a direct result of your choice not to step up, your influence decreases. Your influence on the front lines and with your leaders will be diminished. You are more likely to become reactive and frustrated blaming others for what you have chosen. Blaming others will further reduce your influence.

You first make your choices, then your choices make you.

*"The most valuable player is the one that makes the most players valuable." ~ Peyton Manning*

Excerpt (Ch. 4 of 30) from
## *Blue-Collar Leadership® & Supervision:*
### Unleash Your Team's Potential

# UNDERSTANDING
# ARTIFICIAL INFLUENCE

## THERE IS A DIFFERENCE BETWEEN
## SOMEONE RESPECTING YOUR POSITION
## AND SOMEONE RESPECTING YOU

*"Into the hands of every individual is given a marvelous
power for good or evil - the silent, unconscious, unseen
influence of his life. This is simply the constant radiation
of what man really is, not what he pretends to be."*
~ *William George Jordan*

If you want to begin to lead beyond your position, you
must be respected by those you want to influence. No one
gives you respect. You can demand respect all day long, but it's
a waste of time. I always laugh (on the inside) when I hear
someone demand respect. You will never be respected because
you demand to be respected, at work or at home. It's simply
not going to happen.

Think about it from your own point of view. If there's a
boss or manager you don't like because of who they are as a
person, can they demand respect from you and get it?
Absolutely not. You may respect their position. But, you will
never respect them simply because they demand it. You *must*
respect their position to *keep* your job. But, you don't have to
respect *them* to keep your job.

A position will give you authority but not influence.
Influence must be earned by first earning respect. The more
you are respected the more influence you will gain. Everything
I'm sharing in this book, *if applied*, will help you earn respect
and increase your influence with others.

Having a position or title such as Mom, Dad, Coach, Boss, Supervisor, Manager, VP, President, CEO, Owner, etc. gives you authority and control over other people. I call this *artificial influence*. Artificial influence creates the *illusion* that you have *real* influence. However, if you choose to influence people using only artificial influence, you are not leading. You are simply managing. Sure you may accomplish a lot, but what are you leaving on the table?

You can easily validate the principle of artificial influence by considering those bosses you've had, or now have, that you would never follow if they didn't control your pay, your time off, your promotions, etc. If you only follow a boss because you *have to*, their influence is *not* real. It's artificial. And unfortunately for the company, most likely, you will only do what you have to do.

The title of boss is one that is simply given, often by another manager with artificial influence. However, when it comes to real influence, managers are not in the same league as leaders. If you develop real influence based on character-based principles that you have internalized, then you will *earn* the right to lead. When you do, those reporting to you will do much *more than they have to* simply because they *respect* you.

A high impact leader operates from a position of real influence, not artificial influence or authority.

Listen to the voices of those with *artificial* influence:

- How am I supposed to make something happen when those people don't report to me?
- I can't make them do anything. They don't report to me and won't do anything I tell them to do.
- I can't get anything done in that department. They report to someone else, not me. It's useless to try.
- How can I be responsible for their results when they don't report to me?
- If you want me to make it happen, you've got to give me authority over those people.
- My hands are tied. They don't report to me.

Phrases like those are always spoken by a manager, never

by a leader. I've heard them spoken many times in my career by managers who don't have a clue about leadership. The only influence they have at work is directly tied to the authority, *artificial influence*, which is associated with the position they hold. Without it, they wouldn't accomplish much of anything.

I remember being in a facility as a consultant once. I needed some help from a few team members in a different department, so I asked the manager I was working with if it would be okay if I went over and asked them for some help. He said, *"You'll have to wait. I'll have to get an interpreter because none of them speak English."* I said, *"Okay, I'll go wait over there."* I thought it was interesting. When I got there, they all spoke English to me. Leadership is influence.

Managers make things happen with people who *have to* help them. Leaders make things happen with people who *want to* help them.

Most managers have never read a leadership book and can't understand a leader doesn't need authority to make something happen. Leaders only need *influence* to make something happen. Leadership is *not* about who *has* to help you. Leadership *is* about who *wants* to help you.

Research studies have repeatedly shown a 40% productivity increase when comparing people who *want to* follow a leader with those who *have to* follow a manager.

A manager thrives on artificial influence and is not interested in developing himself or others in order to capture this massive loss of productivity. That's what leaders do, not managers.

How do you influence? What is your style? Are you a director or a connector? Do you tell or sell? What would change if you had more real influence in every situation?

*"When we look at people who disobey their leaders, the first question we ought to ask is not, 'What's wrong with those people?' but rather, 'What's wrong with their leader?' It says that responsibility begins at the top."*
*~ Malcolm Gladwell*

Excerpt (Ch. 26 of 30) from
*Blue-Collar Kaizen:*
*Leading Lean & Lean Teams*

# LEVERAGE THE TEAM

## FOCUS ON STRENGTHS; DEVELOP WEAKNESSES

*"Instead of focusing on weaknesses, give your attention to people's strengths. Focus on sharpening skills that already exist. Compliment positive qualities. Bring out the gifts inherent in them. Weaknesses can wait unless they are character flaws. Only after you have developed a strong rapport with the person and they have begun to grow and gain confidence should you address areas of weakness...and then those should be handled gently and one at a time."*
*~ John C. Maxwell*

High impact Lean leaders have a gift for turning a group of people into a team in a short period of time.

At the start of a kaizen event, calling the group of people a team is a poor use of the word team. They are simply a group of people assembled in a room about to be given a task to accomplish together. Most often, some want to be there, and some don't want to be there. Odds are, this specific group of people has never worked together on a project before.

Knowing about continuous improvement is a must if you're going to lead a kaizen event. However, knowing about continuous improvement (your competency) will not be the key to turning a group of people into a team of people. Turning a group of people into a team of people is about having respect for the people. Your ability to quickly build a strong, functional team will be determined primarily by your character and secondarily by your competency. Your character is key in this area.

I've seen some very talented Lean leaders and others who have an extensive in-depth knowledge of Lean attempt to lead kaizen events. Most often, they struggle from the moment the event kicks off until the end. They know a lot about Lean but very little about leading people effectively. Why? Because their focus has been on learning Lean, not on learning leadership.

When it comes to growing, developing, and creating a new team, high impact Lean leaders know to focus on the team member's strengths in their area of competency and to develop their weaknesses in the area of character.

Each team member's competency strengths (what they know and can do), if leveraged, will launch the team forward. Each team member's character weaknesses (who they are) will hold the team back. This includes you.

High impact Lean leaders know there are always character issues. We all have them. A few of us are constantly working to improving ourselves, but many of us aren't. Focusing on character weaknesses is why high impact Lean leaders blend leadership development and personal growth components into all of their continuous improvement initiatives.

This is why I utilize the 20/80 rule I taught you in chapter 19. I didn't start using it by accident. I started using it by design. Until then, I only focused on leveraging the team's strengths. But, I hadn't been focused on developing their weaknesses. I'm sure you already know the root cause of most major problems that arise during kaizen events, whether with team members or people not on the team, is rooted in character issues.

The majority of Lean leaders focus only on the continuous improvement (competency) component of Lean. As a result, they provide no leadership in the area that will hold them and the team back the most, character development.

The reason Lean leaders do not address character development during kaizen events is because many of them are not addressing it in their own lives. In other words, because they are not leading themselves well, they cannot lead others well. Character development is always the missing link personally and professionally.

In the area of competency, ask questions and generate discussions to find out what people like or don't like to do. Don't assume they like to do what they are paid to do. I always have everyone introduce and speak about themselves before I talk about anything. I ask what their job is, how long they have been with the organization, what their previous job was, what their hobbies are, what they do for fun, how much Lean and event experience they have, and I ask them to tell me about their family.

The answers to these questions and the associated discussions allow me to connect and learn about their strengths. Then, I'm positioned to leverage the team.

*"Humility means knowing and using your strength for the benefit of others, on behalf of a higher purpose. The humble leader is not weak, but strong...is not pre-occupied with self, but with how best to use his or her strengths for the good of others. A humble leader does not think less of himself, but chooses to consider the needs of others in fulfilling a worthy cause. We love to be in the presence of a humble leader because they bring out the very best in us. Their focus is on our purpose, our contribution, and our ability to accomplish all we set out to accomplish." ~ Alan Ross*

Excerpt (Toolbox Tip #15) from
### *Blue-Collar Leadership® Toolbox Tips:*
*60 Micro-Lessons to Maximize Your INFLUENCE*

# 🔧 Toolbox Tip #15

Character counts. Who we are on the inside determines what others see, feel, and experience on the outside.

**Why It Matters:** When it comes to character, it's not about what we know. It's about who we are. People are most often hired for what they know, but they are most often fired for who they are. Our character will either launch us or limit us. Character is personal, but it's not private.

**What We Do:** We intentionally make choices that reveal a high degree of character. We make and keep commitments. We do what we said we would do, when we said we would do it, how we said we would do it, because we said we would do it. We ensure our motive, agenda, and behavior are aligned with positive, character-based principles. We say and do things that build trust.

**What We Don't Do:** We don't lie. We don't make and break commitments. We don't talk about others behind their backs. We don't fail to stand for what's right. We don't hang around negative people. We don't do or say things that create distrust.

**Bad Example(s):** Blaming others for our behavior when things don't go our way. Speaking to others in anger. Pretending to know when we don't know.

### Think About This

"Our reputations do not come from how we talk about ourselves. Our reputations come from how others talk about us." ~ Simon Sinek

Allowing our pride and ego to prevent us from doing the right thing.

**Ask Yourself:** Do I ever blame others for my behavior? Do others control me, or do I control me? Who is responsible for my behavior? What does my behavior communicate to others?

## What Do You Think?

## Order books online at Amazon or TopStoryLeadership.com

High impact leaders align their habits with key values in order to maximize their influence. High impact leaders intentionally grow and develop themselves in an effort to more effectively grow and develop others.

These *10 Values* are commonly understood. However, they are not always commonly practiced. These *10 Values* will help you build trust and accelerate relationship building. Those mastering these *10 Values* will be able to lead with speed as they develop 360° of influence from wherever they are.

## Order books online at Amazon or TopStoryLeadership.com

Are you looking for transformation in your life? Do you want better results? Do you want stronger relationships?

In *Defining Influence*, Mack breaks down many of the principles that will allow anyone at any level to methodically and intentionally increase their positive influence.

Mack blends his personal growth journey with lessons on the principles he learned along the way. He's not telling you what he learned after years of research, but rather what he learned from years of application and transformation. Everything rises and falls on influence.

# Order books online at Amazon or TopStoryLeadership.com

*10 Foundational Elements of Intentional Transformation* serves as a source of motivation and inspiration to help you climb your way to the next level and beyond as you learn to intentionally create a better future for yourself. The pages will ENCOURAGE, ENGAGE, and EMPOWER you as you become more focused and intentional about moving from where you are to where you want to be.

All of us are somewhere, but most of us want to be somewhere else. However, we don't always know how to get there. You will learn how to intentionally move forward as you learn to navigate the 10 foundational layers of transformation.

# Order books online at Amazon or TopStoryLeadership.com

*"Sales persuasion and influence, moving others, has changed more in the last 10 years than it has in the last 100 years. It has transitioned from buyer beware to seller beware" ~ Daniel Pink*

So, it's no longer *"Buyer beware!"* It's *"Seller beware!"* Why? Today, the buyer has the advantage over the seller. Most often, they are holding it in their hand. It's a smart phone. They can learn everything about your product before they meet you. They can compare features and prices instantly. The major advantage you do still have is: YOU! IF they like you. IF they trust you. IF they feel you want to help them.

This book is filled with 30 short chapters providing unique insights that will give you the advantage, not over the buyer, but over your competition: those who are selling what you're selling. It will help you sell yourself.

# Order books online at Amazon or BlueCollarLeadership.com

It's easier to compete when you're attracting great people instead of searching for good people.

*Blue-Collar Leadership® & Culture* will help you understand why culture is the key to becoming a sought after employer of choice within your industry and in your area of operation.

You'll also discover how to leverage the components of The Transformation Equation to create a culture that will support, attract, and retain high performance team members.

*Blue-Collar Leadership® & Culture* is intended to serve as a tool, a guide, and a transformational road map for leaders who want to create a high impact culture that will become their greatest competitive advantage.

# Order books online at Amazon or BlueCollarLeadership.com

*"I wish someone would have given me these books 30 years ago when I started my career on the front lines. They would have launched my career then. They can launch your career now." ~ Mack Story*

*Blue-Collar Leadership®* and *Blue-Collar Leadership® & Supervision* were written specifically for those working on the front lines and those who are leading them. With 30 short, easy to read 3 page chapters, these books contain powerful, yet simple to understand leadership principles and lessons.

*Note: These two Blue-Collar Leadership® books are the blue-collar version of the MAXIMIZE books and contain nearly identical content.*

**Download the first 5 chapters of these books FREE at:
BlueCollarLeadership.com/download**

# Order books online at Amazon or BlueCollarLeadership.com

QUICKLY DEVELOP LEADERS AT EVERY LEVEL

Leaders are BUSY. That's why Mack Story designed *Toolbox Tips*, a collection of powerful leadership principles delivered in a short and easy to understand format for *quick* and *consistent* workforce development.

Kick-off weekly meetings by reviewing a *Toolbox Tip* on **responsibility**, start your team safety meetings with a *Toolbox Tip* on **trust**, or begin your management team meeting with a *Toolbox Tip* on **character**.

Leverage the power of micro-learning with powerful, common-sense leadership principles. Quickly and consistently review, discuss, and apply *Toolbox Tips* to create a leadership culture filled with high impact individuals, high impact team players, and high impact leaders worth following.

# Order books online at Amazon or BlueCollarLeadership.com

The biggest challenge in process improvement and cultural transformation isn't identifying the problems. It's execution: implementing and sustaining the solutions.

*Blue-Collar Kaizen* is a resource for anyone in any position who is, or will be, leading a team through process improvement and change. Learn to engage, empower, and encourage your team for long term buy-in and sustained gains.

Mack Story has over 11,000 hours experience leading hundreds of leaders and thousands of their cross-functional kaizen team members through process improvement, organizational change, and cultural transformation. He shares lessons learned from his experience and many years of studying, teaching, and applying leadership principles.

# Order books online at Amazon or TopStoryLeadership.com

*"I wish someone had given me these books 30 years ago when I started my career. They would have changed my life then. They can change your life now."* ~ Mack Story

*MAXIMIZE Your Potential* will help you learn to lead yourself well. *MAXIMIZE Your Leadership Potential* will help you learn to lead others well. With 30 short, easy to read 3 page chapters, these books contain simple and easy to understand, yet powerful leadership lessons.

*Note: These two MAXIMIZE books are the white-collar, or non-specific, version of the Blue-Collar Leadership® books and contain nearly identical content.*

## ABOUT RIA STORY

Mack's wife, Ria, is also a motivational leadership speaker, author, and a world class coach who has a unique ability to help people develop and achieve their life and career goals and guide them in building the habits and discipline to achieve their personal view of greatness. Ria brings a wealth of personal experience in working with clients to achieve their personal goals and aspirations in a way few coaches can.

Like many, Ria has faced adversity in life. Raised on an isolated farm in Alabama, she suffered extreme sexual abuse by her father from age 12 to 19. Desperate to escape, she left home at 19 without a job, a car, or even a high school diploma. Ria learned to be resilient, and not just survive, but thrive. (Watch her 7 minute TEDx talk at RiaStory.com/TEDx) She worked her way through school, acquiring an MBA with a 4.0 GPA, and eventually resigned from her career in the corporate world to pursue a passion for helping others achieve success.

Ria's background includes more than 10 years in healthcare administration, including several years in management, and later, Director of Compliance and Regulatory Affairs for a large healthcare organization. Ria's responsibilities included oversight of thousands of organizational policies, organizational compliance with all State and Federal regulations, and responsibility for several million dollars in Medicare appeals.

Ria co-founded Top Story Leadership, which offers leadership speaking, training, coaching, and consulting.

## *Ria's Story From Ashes To Beauty*
## by Ria Story

The unforgettable story and inspirational memoir of a young woman who was extremely sexually abused by her father from age 12 to 19 and then rejected by her mother. (Watch 7 minutes of her story in her TEDx talk at RiaStory.com/TEDx)

For the first time, Ria publicly reveals details of the extreme sexual abuse she endured growing up. 13 years after leaving home at 19, she decided to speak out about her story and encourage others to find hope and healing.

Determined to not only survive, but also thrive, Ria shares how she was able to overcome the odds and find hope and healing to Achieve Abundant Life. She shares the leadership principles she applied to find professional success, personal significance, and details how she was able to find the courage to share her story to give hope to others around the world.

Ria states, *"It would be easier for me to let this story go untold forever and simply move on with life…One of the most difficult things I've ever done is write this book. Victims of sexual assault or abuse don't want to talk because they want to avoid the social stigma and the fear of not being believed or the possibility of being blamed for something that was not their fault. My hope and prayer is someone will benefit from learning how I was able to overcome such difficult circumstances. That brings purpose to the pain and reason enough to share what I would rather have left behind forever. Our scars make us stronger."*

Available at Amazon.com in paperback, audio, and eBook. To order your signed copy, to learn more about Ria, or to book her to speak at your event, please visit: **RiaStory.com/TEDx**

# Order books online at Amazon or RiaStory.com

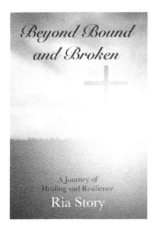

## Ria's Story
*From Ashes To Beauty*

Ria Story

In *Beyond Bound and Broken,* Ria shares how she overcame the shame, fear, and doubt she developed after enduring years of extreme sexual abuse by her father. Forced to play the role of a wife and even shared with other men due to her father's perversions, Ria left home at 19 without a job, a car, or even a high-school diploma. This book also contains lessons on resilience and overcoming adversity that you can apply to your own life.

In *Ria's Story From Ashes To Beauty,* Ria tells her personal story of growing up as a victim of extreme sexual abuse from age 12 – 19, leaving home to escape, and her decision to tell her story. She shares her heart in an attempt to help others overcome their own adversity.

## Order books online at Amazon or RiaStory.com

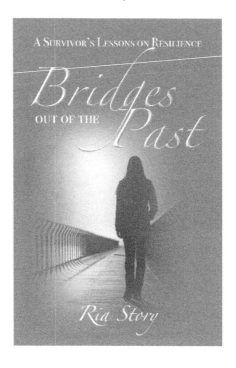

It's not what happens to you in life. It's who you become because of it. We all experience pain, grief, and loss in life. Resilience is the difference between *"I didn't die,"* and *"I learned to live again."* In this captivating book on resilience, Ria walks you through her own horrific story of more than seven years of sexual abuse by her father. She then shares how she learned not only to survive, but also to thrive in spite of her past. Learn how to overcome challenges, obstacles, and adversity in your own life by building a bridge out of the past and into the future.

**(Watch 7 minutes of her story at RiaStory.com/TEDx)**

# Order books online at Amazon or RiaStory.com

You have untapped potential to do, have, and be more in life. But, developing your potential and becoming the best version of yourself will require personal transformation. You will have to transform from who you are today into who you want to become tomorrow.

Gain unique insight in, *"Fearfully and Wonderfully Me: Become the Woman You are Destined to Be"* and the accompanying workbook to help you: believe in yourself and your potential; embrace your self-worth; overcome self-limiting beliefs; increase your influence personally & professionally; and achieve your goals & develop a mindset for success. These two resources will empower you to own your story, write a new chapter, and become the woman and leader you are destined to be.

## Order books online at Amazon or RiaStory.com

You have untapped potential waiting to be unlocked. To be successful requires us to have knowledge of the principles of success, awareness of how to utilize them, and discipline to intentionally apply them. There are no shortcuts to success, but we can travel much faster when we have an achievement model we can apply. This model will help you develop more influence personally and professionally, execute an action plan for personal success, and maximize your potential in life. Both women and men alike will find practical and relevant information to immediately apply to their situation and improve the outcome.

# Order books online at Amazon or RiaStory.com

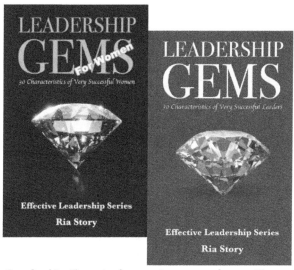

*Note: Leadership Gems is the generic, non-gender specific, version of Leadership Gems for Women. The content is very similar.*

Women are naturally high level leaders because they are relationship oriented. However, it's a *"man's world"* out there and natural ability isn't enough to help you be successful as a leader. You must be intentional.

Ria packed these books with 30 leadership gems which very successful people internalize and apply. Ria has combined her years of experience in leadership roles of different organizations along with years of studying, teaching, training, and speaking on leadership to give you these 30, short and simple, yet powerful and profound, lessons to help you become very successful, regardless of whether you are in a formal leadership position or not.

## Order books online at Amazon or RiaStory.com

Become inspired by this 30-day collection of daily devotions for women, where you will find practical advice on intentionally living with a grateful heart, inspirational quotes, short journaling opportunities, and scripture from God's Word on practicing gratitude.

## Motivational Planning Journals
### Choose a theme for the season of your life!
Now available at Amazon.com or RiaStory.com

Motivational

Purposeful/Living Your Legacy

Productivity

Joy/Faith

Resilience

Make the Most of Today

Start each day with a purposeful mindset, and you will achieve your priorities based on your values.

Just a few minutes of intentional thought every morning will allow you to focus your energy, increase your influence, and make your day all that it can be!

Each journal in the series has different motivational quotes and a motivational theme. Choose one or get all six for an entire year's worth of **Motivational Planning**!

## Order books online at Amazon or RiaStory.com

Ria's *Effective Leadership Series* books are written to develop and enhance your leadership skills, while also helping you increase your abilities in areas like communication and relationships, time management, planning and execution, leading and implementing change. Look for more books in the *Effective Leadership Series*:

- *Straight Talk: The Power of Effective Communication*

- *PRIME Time: The Power of Effective Planning*

- *Change Happens: Leading Yourself and Others through Change (Co-authored by Ria & Mack Story)*

**ENGAGE** Your
# FRONT LINE
To **IMPROVE** the
# BOTTOM LINE!

If you're willing to invest in your
Blue-Collar team, I am too!

~Mack Story

## Limited Time Special Offer:

Take advantage of our "Special Offer Package"
which includes: a greatly reduced speaking fee,
hundreds of FREE books (choose from a mix of
our 32 titles), up to 2 hours of on site speaking or
training, plus we pay all of our expenses. For
current details, visit:
BlueCollarLeadership.com/Special-Offer

*Restrictions apply.*

*"My first words are, GET SIGNED UP! This training
is not, and I stress, not your everyday leadership
seminar!" Sam, VP & COO*

Made in the USA
Monee, IL
10 November 2023

46158195R00085